LETTS HOME DECORATOR

SOFT
FURNISHINGS

HEATHER LUKE

NEW
HOLLAND

First published in 1994
by Charles Letts & Co Ltd
An imprint of
New Holland (Publishers) Ltd
24 Nutford Place
London W1H 6DQ
in association with
Aura Books plc

Reprinted 1996

ISBN 1 85238 539 1

A CIP catalogue record for this book is
available from the British Library.

'Letts' is a registered trademark of
Charles Letts & Co Ltd

Editorial Director: Joanna Lorenz
Project Editor: Lindsay Porter
Design: Millions Design
Photographer: John Freeman
Illustrations: King & King Associates

Designed and edited by
Anness Publishing Ltd
1 Boundary Row
London SE1 8HP

Printed and bound in Singapore

p2: *Bright colours and a
mix of toning prints create
a country feel in this
sunny kitchen.*

CONTENTS

INTRODUCTION

 Making your own soft furnishings is far less difficult than you would imagine, and is immensely satisfying. This book includes projects for all abilities, from simple cushion covers and square tablecloths, to loose covers, blinds and curtains, and illustrates variations and different finishings for further inspiration. Step-by-step instructions demonstrate the techniques involved, and will help you achieve professional results — even if you are attempting soft furnishings for the first time, or are working within a limited budget.

However, soft furnishings are not simply about pinning, tacking and stitching. The choice of fabric, its suitability for the purpose and its relationship to the rest of the room all need careful thought. You will also need to establish the balance and proportions of window treatments to windows, and soft furnishings to hard furnishings. This is far less daunting than it sounds. With a little practice and the help of this book you will be able to devise your own schemes, whether you want to inject a little colour into an existing decor, or plan to make over your entire home.

Opposite *Experiment with tones and textures before developing a room scheme. Here, a colour board was made of neutral tones.*

ASSESSING NEEDS

Successful colour schemes depend on all of the elements in a room being given equal thought and attention to detail. It would be a shame, for instance, to spend the whole budget on an elaborate window treatment, leaving the rest of the room untouched, as this would create a focal point which dominates the room, making it unbalanced and uncomfortable.

Below Fabric swatches in toning colours and contrasting textures can serve as inspiration when devising a room scheme. An alternative may be to keep a board with fabric swatches, cuttings from magazines, sketches and photographs to refer to for ideas.

DESIGN DECISIONS

Consider the points outlined in the Design Checklist, and make lists, cut out ideas from magazines, and find out what is available to buy. Keep a file or inspiration board in your home or office to refer to and pick up ideas from. Make notes about particular colour combinations and textures which you see in other homes, in books and magazines, or on visits to period houses and gardens, noting the things you don't like as well as the things you do. This can be a continuous occupation so that when you are ready to start a project, whether the whole room, the whole house or a single cushion, you already have ideas and information to work from.

Solutions to design problems can be instant and should always be instinctive, but a process of elimination may be helpful for the first stage. Choose your overall style to suit the above criteria and then turn your attention to the detail which will give the project individuality. The extra work involved in adding contrast linings, binding edges or hand-sewn headings will make all the difference, while a good basic scheme can always be added to and revitalized with new accessories, and can move with you.

Work with the room environment : if your present possessions are simple, choose a simple window treatment ; if your room is small and dark, keep it small and dark. Always go with the room – if you try to work against the natural elements of an interior it will be uncomfortable. A room in a cottage will need a fabric and treatment suited to uneven walls and floors, natural textures and earthy colours, whereas a period room will demand stronger and more definite colours and more elegant window treatments. Remember that the amount of light available from differing window sizes and placement within a room, and the ceiling height, will have a dramatic effect on the way in which colour is viewed.

If you are making curtains for a child's room, you will want a simple treatment ; curtains that are easy to pull, fabric that will stand washing and a design that will grow with the child. This does not mean that the curtains have to be boringly practical, quite the opposite, but extra thought and attention to detail are needed. Curtains, for instance, may be hung from a 'curtain pole' made from a simple piece of dowelling, fitted onto coat hooks. Make the curtains from washable cotton with a complementary print used for the edging and lining, with the same print used to make ties for a decorative heading.

PATTERN

Most schemes benefit from the addition of at least one patterned fabric. The scale of the main design, the balance of colours and the background design are the elements that make up a pattern and that determine the eventual use of each. When mixing several patterns, bear in mind that they will work well together as long as there are elements which relate to each other: a unifying colour which runs through all fabrics; similar hues and tones; or scales of design which balance and complement each other. If these elements are present in your selection of fabrics, you cannot go far wrong.

BUILDING A SCHEME

The theory of colour and how colours relate to each other may not at first appear to be relevant to the making of soft furnishings, but a basic knowledge of the origins of each colour and their relationship within the colour wheel will certainly be of great benefit when choosing mixtures of fabrics, whether for edgings and trimmings, for several pieces of furniture which will be close to each other in the same room, or for a choice of prints for tablecloths, napkins etc.

To do this, you will need to know which colours harmonize and which contrast, and be aware not only of the colours which work together, but which tones of those colours work together. You may want to use a colour wheel based on four earth colours and the five traditional decorators' oil colours. The colour wheel illustrated here shows the colours used in their most intense form at the centre, with the earth colours around the outside edge. The colours between show the secondary and tertiary mixes and then the addition of the earth colours.

Variations of a colour are referred to as hues and tones. The *hue* of a colour denotes the balance of the colours which combine to make it, such as one part blue to one part green, or one part blue to two parts green. The *tone* or tonal value of a colour is defined by the amount of white which has been added to it.

All colour schemes should have balanced tones and hues. Working generally within the same band of mixed colours will help you to achieve harmonious blends and create a successful scheme. The three bàsic categories of colour scheme are:

● **monochromatic:** a scheme consisting of a variety of textures and designs in shades of one colour.
● **related:** combinations of tones and hues of colours lying next to each other on the colour wheel.
● **complementary:** combinations of colours from the opposite side of the wheel, ie blue and orange; purple and yellow.

Most room schemes are, in practice, a combination of the above with the hues and tones of colours sensitively balanced to suit the atmosphere and style required.

A simple way to begin to understand and

experiment with colour would be to make a 'neutral' colour board. Use fabrics in neutral shades and of natural materials – wood, brass, brick, straw, metal, ticking, voile, muslin, velvet – to show the interest and warmth which can be created by these easily available colourings and textures.

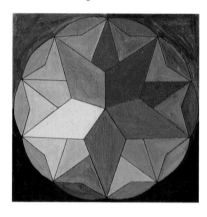

Above *A variation on the colour wheel, based on four earth colours, and five decorator's oil colours.*

Left *Making up a 'neutral' colour board will help you experiment with the interplay of textures.*

Left *You may want to practise building simple colour schemes to understand the relationship between colours. Start with the main elements of the room – the floor, walls, curtains and furniture – all in tones of off-white. Then introduce another colour into the scheme in the form of one chair cover and two cushions. More of the second colour can be added in with printed fabrics and weaves with cushions and a rug in deeper tones.*

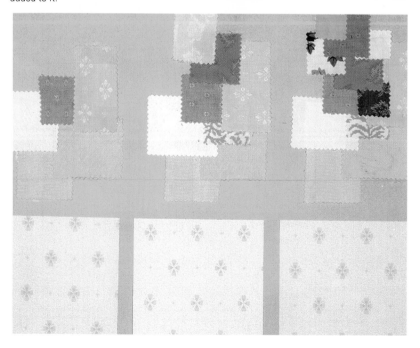

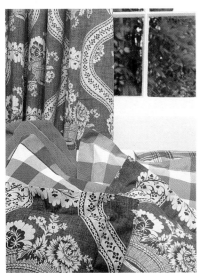

While the main elements remain the same – curtains, cushions, neutral wall colour – the overall picture of any room can be altered according to the balance and mix of colours. The basic scheme comprises six fabrics with varying designs in red, pink and off-white. The tone of the basic scheme is affected by the addition of a complementary colour such as green, or a vivid yellow. A related colour (blue) or a 'neutral' colour such as black will bring out different qualities in the room.

CHOOSING FABRICS

The choice of fabric needs to be considered carefully — there is too much care and time involved in making up soft furnishings to compromise on the main fabric, so be careful to choose the right weave and fibre content to suit your purpose. Remember that an inexpensive fabric such as calico which has been made up well will look unquestionably better than the most expensive fabric which has been badly made up.

You should always handle a piece of your chosen fabric large enough to feel its drape and crushability. When handling fabric ask yourself these questions:

● Does the fabric feel right? Is it crisp enough for straight blinds (shades); warm enough for loose covers; heavy enough to provide insulation?
● How does the fabric drape? Check that it is soft enough, rigid enough, heavy enough or fine enough for its purpose. A fabric which will make a perfect Roman blind will not necessarily have the right draping ability for swags.
● How much will it crease? Take a piece of fabric and crease firmly in one hand. As you open your hand note whether the creases hold; fall out eventually; fall out quickly; do not form at all.

	DESCRIPTION	STRENGTH	SHRINKAGE	VERSATILITY	REMARKS
COTTON	Produced from natural cellulose.	Stronger wet than dry.	Shrinks unless bought pre-shrunk.	Mixes well with most other fibres.	Dyes easily. Easily laundered.
LINEN	Produced from fibres of the flax plant.	Strong; mixed with other fibres to add strength.		Very versatile and easy to work with.	Expensive, therefore often mixed with other fibres. Attractive, because yarn is uneven.
WOOL	Produced from animal fleece.	Strength depends on provenance of wool.	Prone to excessive shrinkage.	Springy texture makes it unsuitable for some uses.	Expensive, so often blended to reduce the price.
SILK	Produced from cocoon of silkworm.	Strong fibres, with good elasticity.		Very versatile.	Expensive, so often blended to reduce the price. Soft, luxurious to touch.
ACRYLIC	Man-made from petrol.	Fibres are not strong; little elasticity.	Does not shrink when fully processed.	Mixes well with wool and cotton.	Inexpensive. Can be heat-set, ie given permanent pleats.
VISCOSE	Produced from wood pulp or animal waste.	Fibres are weak; at their weakest when wet.	Prone to shrinkage.	Mixes well with other natural fibres.	Inexpensive. Easy to dye. Easily laundered.

WEAVES

Fabric is woven on the loom with vertical warp threads fixed in place and the horizontal weft threads woven across, over and under the warp to produce a variety of weaves. The warp is the stronger, thicker thread.

PLAIN WEAVE (1)

The weft threads are woven over one and under one, producing a tight, firm weave. The weight of the fabric is determined by the diameter of the thread and the closeness of the weave.

BASKET WEAVE (2)

The weft threads are woven over two and under two, producing a strong, loose weave with more drape than plain weave.

TWILL (3)

The weft threads are woven over one and under two or more, creating a pattern of diagonal lines.

LOOPED (TOWELLING) (4)

Often made from cotton or a cotton mix, this is produced with a warp pile and additional yarn in loops to form a thick pile.

HERRINGBONE (5)

This is a twill weave which is broken to produce vertical stripes.

FELT (6)

Short wool fibres (known as staple), unsuitable for weaving, are wetted, heated and put under pressure so that the scales on the outside of each fibre are agitated and lock into one another, producing a flat, even, matted cloth. Fabric of varying rigidity is produced depending on the type of wool used.

VELVET (7)

Originally 100% silk, now made from cotton, viscose or other man-made fibres. Yarn loops woven into the warp produce a dense, thick pile.

SATIN STRIPE (8)

The weft threads are woven over two or more warp threads and under one, producing a very hard wearing cloth with a slight sheen.

DOBBY (9)

An attachment (a dobby) added to the plain weave loom misses out warp threads to form a simple geometric pattern.

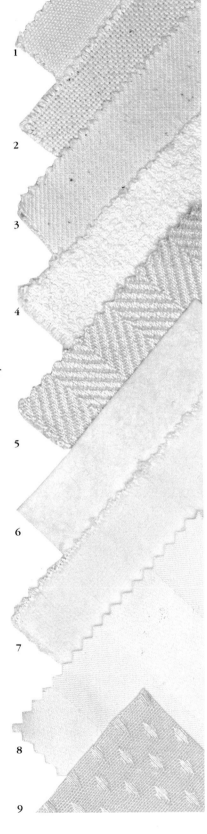

1
2
3
4
5
6
7
8
9

GLOSSARY OF FABRICS

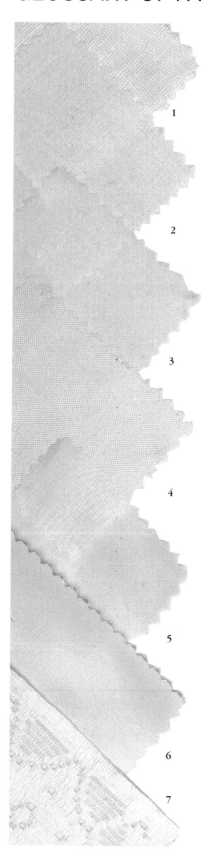

MUSLIN (1)

A white or off-white, open-weave cloth which can be dyed in pastel colours. Inexpensive. Use with at least triple fullness for floaty bed drapes and under-curtains to diffuse light. Layers of muslin will gather easily for interesting window treatments but will form pleats if hung in a damp atmosphere for any period of time.

CALICO (LIGHTWEIGHT) (2)

The lighter weight of this plain weave cotton makes it suitable for inexpensive curtains and bed drapes, and for making up patterns for loose covers.

ORGANZA (3)

Similar to organdie and made of silk, polyester or viscose. Very springy, used for stiffened headings of fine fabrics. Its crisp texture allows it to be made up into Roman blinds (shades) to filter light and insects and to protect the main curtains. An interesting effect can be achieved by using layers of varying tones or colours over each other.

VOILE (4)

Fine, light, plain-weave cotton or polyester fabric dyed in many plain colours. Use for filmy curtains, bed drapes and under-curtains. Washes easily and usually needs little pressing. Silk and wool voiles can be used for fine drapery.

ORGANDIE (5)

The very finest cotton fabric, usually from Switzerland. An acid finish gives organdie a unique crispness. Use for lightweight curtains and dressing tables, alone or over a coloured lining. Organdie can be used to make lovely pleated and butterfly-frilled edgings, and pleated lampshades. Washable, but needs to be pressed damp.

TAFFETA (6)

Ordinarily woven from silk, now made from acetate and blends. A plain-weave fabric with light-catching properties resulting from weaving fibres with a sheen. Suitable for elaborate drapes because of its light reflecting qualities and because it handles well. Unsuitable for covers and upholstery. Interesting checked patterns can be made by weaving varying hues and tones of colours together.

LACE (7)

Any open-work cloth in designs ranging from simple spots to elaborate panels. Usually in cotton or a cotton and polyester mixture. If washable, use for bed drapes, under-curtains, or as a protection to the main curtains. Simple designs are sold by the metre or yard, and more elaborate designs are often sold as panels or lambrequins.

Handmade lace can be bought, but it is very expensive, so mass-produced machine-woven lace will almost always be used for furnishing.

CALICO (1)
Named after Calicut in India where it was first produced. A coarse, plain-weave cotton in cream or white with 'natural' flecks in it. Available in many widths and weights. Use for inexpensive curtains, bed drapes or garden awnings. To ensure fabric has shrunk to its full extent, wash before use and press while damp as calico creases easily.

HOLLAND (2)
A plain-weave, firm, hard-wearing fabric made from cotton or linen stiffened with oil or shellac. Most useful for blinds (shades) to protect fabrics fading in the sunlight. Holland can be used for curtaining and looks especially good as main curtains with under-curtains of muslin or calico.

HESSIAN (JUTE) (3)
A coarse plain-woven fabric made from jute or a jute and hemp mix, in various weights and available in many colours. Use for sacking or upholstery or use the finer weaves for making curtains and blinds (shades). Usually washable but wash before making up to check shrinkage.

SAILCLOTH (4)
A very stiff, hard-wearing fabric in plain or basket weave made from 100% cotton or a cotton/polyester mix. Can be used in its natural colour for furnishings or for inexpensive curtains, or coloured and striped for garden awnings and deck chairs. Iron while damp as sailcloth creases easily.

CAMBRIC (5)
A closely woven plain-weave fabric with a sheen on one side, made from linen or cotton. Use, wash and press as for calico. Cambric is widely used for cushion pad covers as the close weaves prevent feathers creeping through.

SILK SHANTUNG (6)
Light- to mediumweight silk, woven with irregular yarns to give a dull, rough appearance. Available in an extensive range of colours. Gathers and frills well, for very feminine treatments and finishes. Use for curtains, cushions, light drapes and lampshades.

SILK NOILE (7)
Light- to mediumweight silk in a natural colour, with small pieces of the cocoon woven in as flecks. Relatively inexpensive, use interlined for heavy curtains and slip covers, or unlined for lightweight summer curtains and cushions.

TICKING (8)
Originally a fine striped woven linen used for covering feather mattresses as its characteristic tight, herringbone weave repelled feathers. Originally in black and white, ticking is now woven in many colours and weights. Use for curtains and upholstery, for slip covers and as a lining for boxes and suitcases. Not usually pre-shrunk so wash before using to check shrinkage.

CANVAS (9)
Often called cotton duck. A plain-weave cotton in various weights, available as unbleached, coarse cotton or more finely-woven and dyed in strong colours. Suitable for upholstered chair covers, inexpensive curtains, slip covers, and outdoor use.

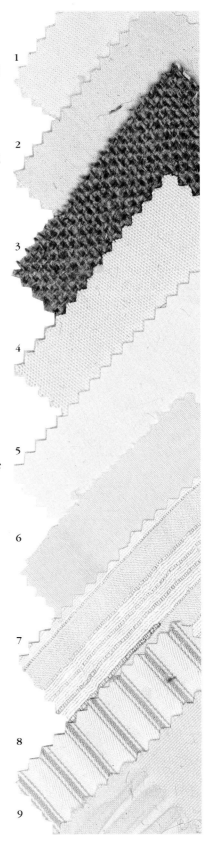

CORDUROY (1)
A strong cotton fabric woven to form vertical ribs by floating extra yarn across the warp which is then cut to make the pile. Press on a velvet pinboard while still damp. Use for traditional upholstery.

TAPESTRY (2)
Originally a hand-woven fabric with a ribbed surface in many colours. Now used to describe heavy, stiff fabrics woven in several layers. Use for heavy-duty upholstery and heavy curtains.

BROCADE (3)
A traditionally-woven fabric using silk, cotton, wool or mixed fibres, made on a jacquard loom, in a multi- or self-coloured floral design. Traditional motifs include cherubs, vases, ribbons, bunches of flowers etc. A true brocade has additional coloured weft threads which float on the back and are brought forwards onto the front to produce the pattern on the right side. Some brocades are washable but most will need dry cleaning. Brocades drape well and can be used for curtains, traditional bed drapes, loose covers and upholstery.

JACQUARD (4, 7)
The design of the finished cloth is woven into the threads. Jacquard was originally machine-made using a punchcard system with variations of weaving techniques to form a reversible pattern. Although the process is now computerized it is slow and therefore expensive.

DAMASK (5, 6)
A jacquard fabric first woven in Damascus with satin floats on a warp satin background. Woven in cotton, silk, wool and mixed fibres in various weights. Most damasks are self-coloured. The surface design will run in a different direction to the background and the face cloth will have a sheen, so damask cloths can be made up reversed if a matt finish is required. May be dry cleaned or washed depending on the fibre content. Use for curtains, bed drapes, loose covers and upholstery.

CREWEL (8, 9)
A plain- or hopsack-woven, natural cotton background embroidered in chain stitch in plain cream wool or multi-coloured wools. Originally a ladies' hobby producing embroidered bed covers and bed hangings, now mostly handmade in India in floral and Eastern designs. Use for curtains, bed covers, loose covers and upholstery.

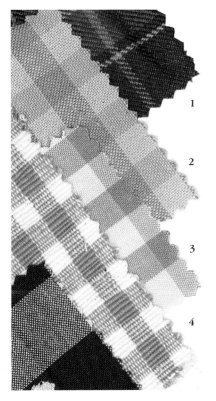

1

2

3

4

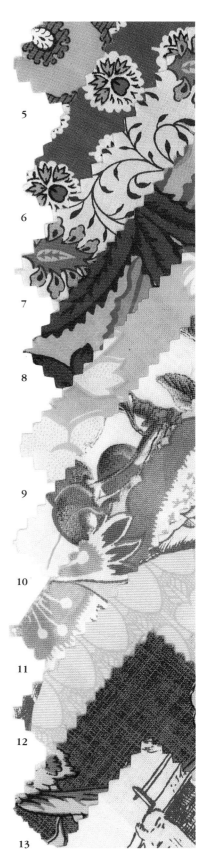

5

6

7

8

9

10

11

12

13

INDIENNES (5, 6, 7, 8)

During the mid-17th century, Parisians imported richly printed cloths ('toiles peintes') from India. By 1675 these cloths were printed in Nimes and Avignon using carved blocks to print natural dyes onto calico. The distinctive designs were soon adapted for decorative home accessories. These are now known as 'Provençal' prints, and can be used in country-style kitchens as curtains, tablecloths etc.

PRINTED DAMASK (9)

An extra textural dimension is added to the print by weaving the design into the actual fabric (see Damask).

CHINTZ (10, 11)

Traditionally a cotton fabric with an Eastern design featuring flowers and birds, often with a resin finish giving a characteristic sheen which repelled dirt. Now mostly used to describe any patterned or plain glazed fabric. The glaze will eventually wash out so dry clean only. Use for curtains, upholstery and loose covers.

TOILE DE JOUY (12, 13)

Created in France in 1770 featuring pastoral designs in one colour printed onto calico cloth from India using copper-plate printing techniques. Different patterns and hues can be mixed together very effectively. Use for curtains, loose covers, upholstery, cushions, bedding etc. Use *en masse* or on a small piece of period upholstered furniture in a chintz room.

TARTAN (1)

Authentic tartans belong to individual Scottish clans and are woven or worsted fine twill weaves with an elaborate checked design. Both warp and weft have threads with mixed colours. Tartan designs are now also made in silk to produce elegant shimmering fabrics. Traditional wool tartans are hard-wearing and suitable for upholstering sofas and chairs, curtains and cushions. Use in study-type rooms or as a contrast in a chintzy floral room.

GINGHAM (2, 3, 4)

A plain-weave fabric with equal stripes of white, plus one other colour in both warp and weft threads to produce blocks of checks or stripes. Usually 100% cotton or a cotton mix. Use for small windows in cottage-style rooms, kitchens and children's bedrooms, and for loose covers.

SOFT MATERIALS

HEAVYWEIGHT INTERLINING (1)
Use interlining to improve the hang of
your curtains and for insulation.

MEDIUM INTERLINING (2, 3)

DOMETTE (4)
A very fine cotton interlining for use in
very lightweight curtains. Available
white or unbleached.

SARILLE (5)
An inexpensive synthetic interlining of
light to medium weight.

MILIUM (FRONT) (6)
A lining with a backing of aluminium
thread to insulate and block light.

MILIUM (BACK) (7)

BLACK-OUT CLOTH (8)
Fabric which prevents any light
penetration. Use only with dark
background curtain fabric.

CURTAIN LINING (9, 10)
Available in cream or white.

CURTAIN HEADING TAPE (11, 30, 31)
Available in 2.5–7.5 cm (1–3 in)
standard widths. Used to stiffen hand-
gathered and pleated headings and
smocked headings.

INDIA TAPE (12)
Use for ties at bed valance (dust ruffle)
corners, headboard loose covers and
for informal tied headings on
lightweight curtains.

CHAIN WEIGHT (13)
Use a lightweight chain in the hems of
heavy curtains to add weight.

BLIND (SHADE) CORD (14)
Use for Roman, festoon, Austrian and
cascade blinds (shades). Also useful for
pulling through rouleau loops.

PIPING CORD (15, 16)
Use for making piping (cord) for loose
covers and cushions, and for decorative
edges on tablecloths.

CURTAIN HOOKS (17)
Use for hand sewing.

PENNY WEIGHT (18)
To weight the corners of curtains.

BRASS CURTAIN (CURLY) HOOKS (19)
Use for heading tapes as white plastic
hooks discolour and become brittle.

PIN HOOKS (20)
Use to fix into stiffened hand-pleated
headings.

BRASS RINGS (21, 24)
Use 1.25 cm (½ inch) solid brass rings
for blind (shade) cords. Plastic rings are
less visible but will perish in sunlight.

CALICO (22)
Use for fabric toiles as a pattern for the
main fabric, plain curtains or loose
covers.

DACRON (23)
Use for quilting bedcovers, and
covering foam cushions between the
foam and the lining cover.

PENCIL PLEAT TAPE (25)
A quick method for pelmet (valance)
headings and for curtain headings that
will remain closed.

GATHERING TAPE (26, 27, 28)
The most useful sizes are 1–2 cm (½–1
in). Machine or hand stitch and pull up
the tapes to form gathered headings.

BUCKRAM (29)
Use to stiffen headings before hand
pleating, especially for triple pleats,
goblet pleats etc.

ZIP (32)
Use light-, medium- or heavyweight
zips in white, cream or the main fabric
colour.

POPPER TAPE (33)
Use for closures for box cushions and
loose covers.

VELCRO (34)
Use to fit pelmets (valances) to pelmet
(valance) board fronts. Velcro is too
bulky to be used as a closure for
cushions or for curtain headings.

TOOLS AND EQUIPMENT

IRON (1)
Buy the heaviest domestic iron possible and keep filled with water to maximize the weight. It should be able to reach a high temperature and have steam and spray controls.

CURTAIN CLIPS (2)
Use large bulldog clips to hold the fabrics on the table and prevent them moving until stitched.

RULER (3)
A metre rule or yardstick is needed for measuring fabric and accurate lengths.

PIN CUSHION (4)
Keep a large pin cushion on the table and a small wrist pin cushion to use at the machine and away from the table.

SEWING MACHINE (5)
You will need a sturdy, basic machine with forward and reverse stitches. A swing needle may be useful but is not necessary. You will need a normal stitching foot plus a piping (cord) foot and a zipper foot.

PINS (6)
Use fine steel mediumweight pins for general use, and heavy pins for loose covers and heavy fabrics.

TAPE MEASURE (7)
This should be made of linen, glass-fibre or other non-stretching fabric.

NEEDLES (8)
Available in many sizes – keep a variety to use with different weights of fabric.

MARKERS (9)
Use a marking pen (or pencil) which will rub off the fabric easily.

CORNER TURNER (10)
A plastic or bone tool for creasing and turning points.

STITCH RIPPER (11)
For unpicking mistakes.

THREAD (12)
Always match thread with fabric – cotton with cotton, silk with silk etc. Either cotton or silk may be used for wool.

SET SQUARE (13)
This should be at least 60 cm × 30 cm (24 in × 12 in). Use for squaring fabric sides and hems.

SKEWERS (14)
Use upholstery skewers to hold heavy fabrics in place on the work table and to hold drapery in place while cutting.

THIMBLE (15)
This is essential to protect fingers when working with several layers of fabric and very heavy fabrics.

STAPLER (16)
Buy a heavyweight stapler for fixing velcro to pelmet boards (cornices), and for upholstered headboards.

GAUGE (17)
A small ruler with a marker that can be set will ensure accurate turnings.

SCISSORS (18)
For cutting, use heavy scissors with a 20–22 cm (8–9 in) blade.
   For snipping, use a small pair with 7–10 cm (3–4 in) blades.
   Pinking shears are useful for attractive edgings and to prevent fraying.

CURTAINS

Effective window treatments will help to set the scene in any interior — whether gauzy unlined curtains for a country bedroom, or lush velvet curtains with a gathered pelmet (valance). The following pages will tell you everything you need to know about planning, measuring and making curtains, with instructions for hem and heading variations.

Below A single, unlined curtain is held with a tie-back and rosette of the same fabric. The net curtain underneath acts as a lining, which can hang free to filter sunlight when the main curtain is drawn back.

MEASURING WINDOWS

When you are considering the most appropriate treatment for your room, look for anything around the window which might influence the position of the curtain fitting – there may be pipes which would be better hidden behind the curtains, or electrical wires which will prevent fixing into a particular area. Window sills may project further than you would wish; radiators may extend either side of the window and need to be hidden at the sides; or beams may be in awkward places – right above one corner of the window, cutting into the centre, and so on.

Cut templates around anything that might be in the way, so that the headings of curtains or pelmets (valances) can be cut around the obstacle if necessary and the fittings adjusted accordingly. Cornices should usually be above the curtaining, but sometimes the side of the pelmet will·need to return onto the cornice. If this is the case, make a template of the cornice shape so that the side can be cut to fit exactly.

Now look at the actual window. Measure and note the positions of any fittings which will need to be covered, such as those for double glazing and blinds (shades). Decide whether you need blinds and/or pelmets to cover unsightly objects around the area and how and exactly where they should be fitted.

Measure from the top of the frame or reveal to the floor and from the ceiling (or under the cornice) to the top of the window and from the ceiling to the floor. Measure at least three times across the width of each window so that you are aware if the floor slopes. Measure the width of the window, noting any possible problems. Measure the distance available all around the window for stack-back and to avoid pictures, bookcases, etc. Curtain fixings must always be exactly level (use a spirit level when fitting and if necessary when measuring as well) so hem adjustments may need to be made if the floor slopes in an old house.

The recess measurements for blinds should be taken at several positions for the finished width and height. Again check for obstacles such as TV or telephone sockets. Blinds must hang straight so use a spirit level and make adjustments if window frames are uneven.

Right Accessories enhance a simple window treatment: the pole and rings, and bound edge on the gathered heading suit the scheme, both in terms of colour and style.

Below Architectural details are not as difficult to accommodate as you would imagine – cut a template to size around awkward corners.

CURTAIN FIXTURES

Left *Simplicity is the key when dressing small windows – a striped cotton curtain with bound edges and toning lining is threaded onto a wooden pole.*

For most uses, the best tracks (rods) are metal with plastic runners (less noisy than metal runners) with a pull cording system wholly enclosed within the track. These tracks are available in several different qualities to suit the weight and length of your curtains.

Some of these tracks are available ready packed with all fittings and are telescopic so they can be adjusted to fit windows of different widths. If these will not meet your requirements, a specialist track supplier will make up any track to your measurements, and will be willing to advise you on problem windows.

There are other tracks available for specific uses: those which bend around an archway; self-supporting tension rods for recesses; or tracks designed to hold voile curtains. They are available in a number of standard colours, or with brass finishes.

Bay windows will need special attention. Metal tracks of any weight can be bent to fit around any bay window – whether three-sided, five-sided, seven-sided, or semi-circular. Again, ask your specialist curtain fittings supplier to measure up and bend the track for you, as this requires a special tool to prevent the side caving in and stopping the runners moving freely.

CORDING

Cording is essential with interlined and long curtains. You do not want to clean curtains any more than is absolutely necessary and if curtains are pulled by hand they will inevitably become marked on the leading edges – unless white gloves are worn on all occasions!

The cording set should be enclosed within the track (rod) to prevent the curtain hooks catching the cords and jamming the system. The overlap arm on metal tracks is neat and does not project any further forwards than is necessary to allow the curtains to overlap. Plastic overlaps are less attractive, and their bulkiness often ruins the smooth hanging of the curtains in the centre of the window.

The cords can be cut and weighted with brass weights, available in a variety of sizes to suit your curtains. A brass S-clip will hold the cords apart and prevent them twisting together. Or, if you prefer, the pull cord can be held taut with a tension pulley attached to the skirting or sill behind the curtain, which holds the cord in a continuous loop. This is especially useful when the width of the track is of a greater distance than the height, because if the cords were cut and weighted, there would always be one cord too short and one trailing.

FITTINGS

Tracks (rods) can be fitted to the wall or to the ceiling, and most fittings are suitable for both uses. Always drill a hole large enough and long enough to ensure that the fitting is secure. The packaged tracks (rods) will include the screws, but 6.5 cm (2½ in) screws and the equivalent plugs will be sufficient to secure most fittings.

The side fittings which hold the track to the wall are available in several different sizes so that the track can be fitted at different distances to the wall, allowing the curtains to hang straight over a radiator or deep sill if necessary. A deeper fitting also allows space for a blind (shade) to fit in behind the curtains. Use centre fittings as often as is recommended for your weight of track and curtaining. Never try to economize here or you will probably have to re-fit the entire track!

POLES

If you prefer to hang your curtains from poles you need to consider which would be most appropriate to the finished style. So many variations of pole finishes and finial style are available that any combination is possible. You may choose a cherrywood pole with an ebony line for a Grecian look, or a chunky pole with a country-style paint finish for a rustic look – or anything in between.

In any situation, the style must suit the room and the curtaining. A long, heavy curtain will need a chunky, solid pole and proportionate finials. Conversely a small cottage window will need a much smaller pole. A specialist curtain supplier will stock a far greater variety than the rather limited 'off the peg' styles available in department stores, so ask for advice rather than compromise on your ideal choice.

The best wall brackets to use are those which will hold the curtain pole and the curtains as near to the wall as possible. They should have fixing points above and below the pole, with three fixing points on the side and two at the centre.

Below Curtain fittings – rings, poles and appropriate brackets – come in a wide range of materials, colours and styles, and are an integral part of the window treatment. Specialist suppliers should be able to advise if you have particular requirements.

ESTIMATING FABRIC

The first step to estimating fabric is to decide how you want the curtains to look. Consider the position and height of the fitting, and the amount of space at either side of the window. The finished length, fullness, edgings or trimmings required, heading style and type of fitting to be used will all need to be decided before accurate estimates can be made.

There are two length measurements used in making up curtains – the 'hook' drop and the 'overall' drop. The hook drop is the measurement from the top of the curtain hook (or the bottom of the fitting through which the hook will hold) to the finished length, and the overall drop includes any distance above the hook, ie from the very top of the curtain to the finished length.

If your calculations have to accommodate a pattern repeat, note the amount of spare fabric left over, and decide how best to use it. If there is only a little spare you might decide to alter the headings – to have a frilled and bound heading rather than bound only, or to increase the heading fullness from frilled to bunched. If there is more fabric available it could be used to make matching cushions, cushion frills, tie-backs or pelmets (valances).

Planning the fabric in the way indicated on the following pages means that you will never have wasted pieces, and will be aware when cutting of the importance of using the fabric wisely.

If you are working with an expensive fabric and the estimated cuts were just over a whole repeat (ie 4.1 repeats) you might decide to shorten the hem or heading allowance just enough to save costs without damaging the hanging quality.

Always add an extra repeat to the total amount of fabric estimated to allow you to start your hemline in the position on the pattern which you choose, rather than the random start point of the piece purchased.

CALCULATING CURTAIN LENGTHS

1 Calculate the hook drop as accurately as possible. The fittings should be in place *before* the curtains are finished so that an accurate hook drop and overall drop can be obtained. Allow for all measurements above and below the curtains, including possible new flooring, depth of carpet etc.

example

ceiling to floorboards	270 cm (108 in)
less allowance for carpet of 2 cm (¾ in)	268 cm (107¼ in)
less allowance for pelmet board (cornice) of 2 cm (¾ in)	266 cm (106½ in)
plus overlong allowance of 5 cm (2 in)	271 cm (108½ in)
Overall drop	**271 cm (108½ in)**

2 Add the appropriate hem and heading allowances to the overall drop.

example

hem	12 cm (5 in)
heading	20 cm (8 in)
Each cut length	**303 cm (121½ in)**

3 For patterned fabrics it is important to calculate each cut length so that the pattern matches correctly and prevents unnecessary wastage of fabric. Divide the cut length by the length of the pattern repeat of the fabric, and allow up to the next full repeat for each cut.

example

finished length	303 cm (121½ in)
divided by repeat of 65 cm (26 in)	4.66
Round up to next pattern repeat	**5**

4 Multiply the number of repeats needed by the pattern repeat.

example

5 × 65 cm (26 in)	325 cm (130 in)
Each cut length will be 325 cm (130 in)	

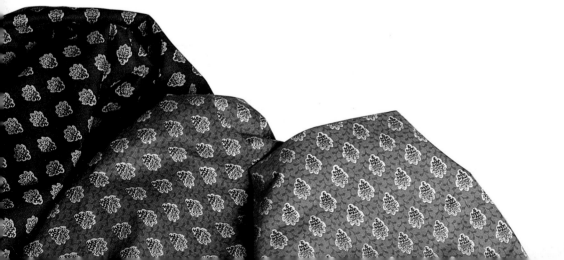

CALCULATING CURTAIN WIDTHS

1 **Fitting length.** A classically proportioned window will be twice as tall as it is wide. You may want to take this into account when establishing the length of the fitting, and how far it should extend either side of the window. This length is known as the stack-back, and is usually between 15–30 cm (6–12 in) either side of the window.

2 **Return.** This is the side piece of the curtain which covers the distance between the end of the fitting and the wall. An average return for a pole fitting is 6–10 cm (2¼–4 in); for a lath, 4–8 cm (1½–3¼ in), and for a pelmet board (cornice) 12–18 cm (4½–7 in).

3 **Overlap.** The size of the centre curtain overlap is defined by the type of fitting used. A non-corded pole will have no built-in overlap facility, so an allowance of 5–6 cm (2–2½ in) per curtain should be made, for ease in closing. A pull-corded track will have a built-in facility of 10–12 cm (4–4½ in). The overlaps on plastic tracks are bulky and impractical to use, and are best avoided. A hand pleated heading should be planned so that the overlap will come within two pleats, without destroying the balance of the pleating.

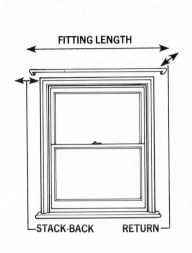

FITTING LENGTH

STACK-BACK   RETURN

4 To calculate the widths needed add the fitting length and return and divide in half. Add the required overlap to each of the curtains.

ESTIMATING HEMS AND HEADING

The following charts will enable you to estimate quickly the amount of extra fabric needed for different hems and headings. Once you have calculated the finished drop and width, including stack-backs, return and overlap, multiply the fabric width by the following figures to accommodate the extra fullness required for each heading.

The fullness allowance can be reduced for short curtains which need less 'weight' to hang well. If space is restricted for stack-back, pleats can be made to the least fullness in the scale. Sometimes if the curtain fabric is very heavy or of a design which needs to be seen hanging as 'flat' as possible, just 1.5 times the fabric fullness will be sufficient.

For hem and heading allowances lengthwise, simply add to the finished drop the extra length required. This is a general guide and individual situations may need adaptation.

HEMS AND HEADING ALLOWANCE	
Heading allowance	
Bound	no extra fabric
Bunched	3 × finished heading length average: 35 cm (14 in)
Frilled	2 × length of frill + 1.5 cm (¾ in) average: 16 cm (6½ in)
Goblet	length of pleat × 2 average: 28 cm (11 in)
Pencil pleat	length of pleat average: 8 cm (3¼ in)
Smocked	length of gather average: 6 cm (2¼ in)
Triple pleat	length of pleat × 2 average: 24 cm (9½ in)
Hem allowance	
Unlined curtains	16 cm (6½ in)
Lined curtains	16 cm (6½ in)
Lined, bound hems, plain lining	8 cm (3¼ in)
Lined, bound hems, contrast lining	no extra fabric
Interlined curtains	12 cm (5 in)
Voile curtains	8–12 cm (3¼–5 in)

FULLNESS ALLOWANCE	
Folded headings	
Slotted	2.00–3.00
Voiles	2.50–3.00
Gathered headings	
Bunched	2.25–2.50
Hand-sewn	2.50–3.00
Pencil pleat	2.50–2.75
Smocked	2.50–3.50
Tape	1.75–2.25
Ties	1.25–2.50
Hand-pleated headings	
Goblets	2.25–2.50
Triple (French)	2.25–2.75

Left *Unlined curtains with bound headings hang from wooden rings. The brass fittings add a touch of formality.*

DRESSING CURTAINS

Hand-headed curtains need to be dressed as soon as they are hung so that the pleats are trained to fall evenly. A little patience at this stage — you will need to be able to leave the curtains tied back for at least 48 hours and possibly up to 96 hours depending on the fabric — will ensure that your curtains will always hang well and the pleats will fall into place each time the curtains are pulled.

With the curtains in the stack-back position, make sure that the heading is in order with the pleats forward and the gaps folded evenly between each pleat. These gaps will be folded either behind or in front of the pleats depending on the fitting and the heading style. If the curtain hangs under a track or pole, the gaps will fold behind, if in front of a pole, the gaps will be folded to the front. Headings such as goblet pleats will only look their best if the gaps are behind.

Stand on a step ladder so you are at eye level with the headings. Take the fabric from each pleat and smooth down through the curtain as far as you can reach to form each pleat into a separate fold.

Now standing on the floor or lower down the step ladder, starting at the leading edge, follow these pleats through to waist height. Fold each pleat evenly and tie a tape or strip of fabric loosely around the curtain to hold the pleats in place.

Kneeling on the floor, follow the folds through into the hem and finger press firmly. Heavily interlined curtains need to have this fold formed very firmly, or the hem will wrinkle quite badly within each fold. If the curtains are overlong, keep the pleats

together and bend the curtain out to one side.

Tie another tape or strip of fabric around the curtain hems to hold the pleats in place. If the curtains are very long, tie in one or two more places. Check that the pleats are hanging comfortably. If one or two seem twisted, adjust them and re-pleat completely if necessary. Springy fabrics may need to be re-adjusted several times, but will become easier as the pleats are trained. The ties should be loose enough not to mark the fabric, but nonetheless tight enough that they do not fall down.

UNLINED CURTAINS

Unlined curtains are the simplest form of window covering to make. If you are unsure of your skills or are tackling home furnishings for the first time, this is a good place to start. Choose an inexpensive fabric such as muslin or calico, make up carefully with an interesting heading and fixing, and both your confidence and curtain-making skills will increase dramatically.

Use unlined curtains in a lightweight voile, muslin or calico to disguise an ugly view; as a door curtain to discourage insects in the summer months; for filmy, floaty bed drapes or long curtains; or for curtains which need constant washing. In a city home, easily washed under-curtains are essential for preventing dirt penetrating into more formal drapes. Pretty unlined, lightweight curtains are a more individual, softer interpretation of the old fashioned 'net curtain'.

1 Estimate the number of widths of fabric you will need for each curtain (very fine fabrics should be three times the width of the window). Calculate the finished drop and add 16 cm (6½ in) for the hem plus heading allowance.

Cut out the lengths. Trim away selvedges and any writing. Join widths with a French seam or make a flat seam, neatened by turning under 0.5 cm (¼ in) on each side to the wrong side and stitching. Always join two half widths to either side of a full width to avoid a centre seam.

2 Working on a flat surface, turn in both side edges 6 cm (2¼ in) to the wrong side, and press. Re-open the turnings and fold in half to give double thickness. Pin and press. Turn up the hem 16 cm (6½ in) and press. Re-open and fold in half as before, pin and press. Position a temporary pin exactly through the point of the corner.

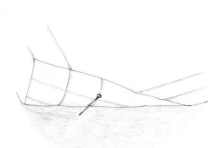

3 Open out all folds and turn in the corner so the pin is visible.

4 Refold the sides and hem along the pressed lines. Make sure that the pin is still on the point and the fabric is lying flat inside. Pin and press.

5 Neatly slip stitch both sides and hem, inserting a fabric weight at each corner and seam. Stitch the mitre with tiny neat stitches.

6 Lay the curtain on a flat surface, making sure that there are no creases in the fabric. Using a long ruler, measure up from the hem to your finished drop and mark with a pin. Repeat this six times across each width of fabric, starting just inside each edge and including each seam. Fold fabric over to the wrong side along the marked line and stitch your chosen heading.

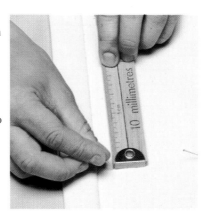

LINED CURTAINS

Lined curtains will give a more finished look than unlined curtains, and can be made up in a variety of fabrics. Delicate silks will be more substantial with the addition of a lining, and the drape of heavier fabrics will improve. Remember to look beyond the actual curtain material when dressing the window – consider the effect of different headings, tie-backs and accessories for a look that is completely yours.

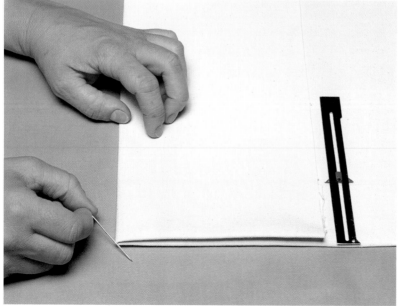

1 Join widths of main fabric and press seams open. Always join two half widths either side of a whole width to avoid a centre seam. Trim away selvedges neatly. Repeat with lining, then turn up 5 cm (2 in) twice to give a double hem, pin and press. Neatly sew along the top of the hem to hold in place. Press and put lining to one side.

2 Lay the curtain fabric flat on the table and press thoroughly to remove any creases. Turn in the side seams of the curtain 6 cm (2¼ in) each, pin and press. Turn up the hem 16 cm (6½ in), ensure that the pattern runs evenly across the width, and press.

3 Open out the fold and refold in half, to produce a double hem. Pin and press. Position a temporary pin exactly through the point of the corner. To mitre both bottom corners, open out the folds and turn in the corner so that the pin is visible.

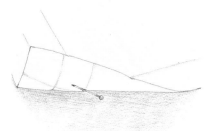

4 Refold the sides and hems along the original fold lines, and mitre the corner so that the side and hem turnings line up. Ensure that the pin is once again on the point and the fabric is lying flat inside. Pin and press.

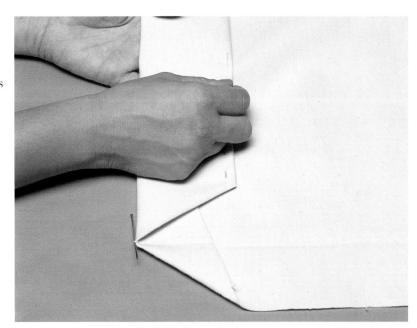

5 Using even stitches, neatly herringbone down both sides of the curtain and remove all pins. Picking up only one thread at a time, loosely slip stitch the hem, stitching a weight into each seam. Ladder stitch both mitres, slipping a weight into each corner. Remove all pins. ▶

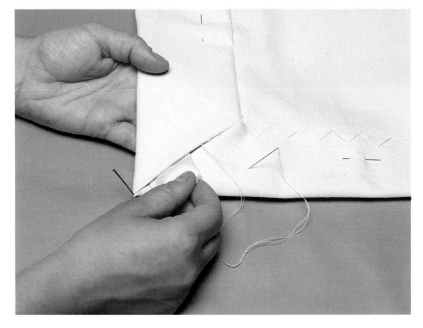

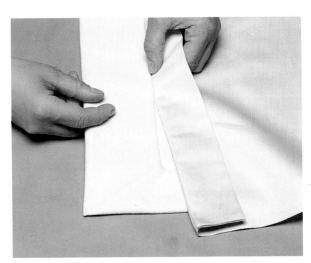

6 Using the pre-prepared curtain linings, place lining on top of the curtain, wrong sides together. Ensure that the seams match exactly and the top of the lining hem lines up with the top of the curtain hem.

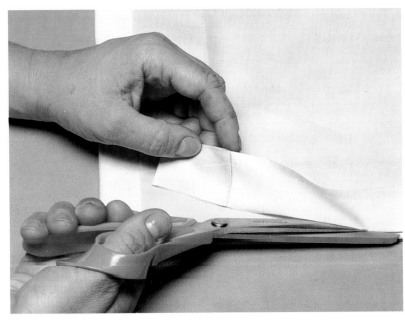

7 Turn back the lining and lock-in along seams, and twice across the width at equal distances, using the same colour thread as the main fabric. Reposition the lining and smooth out. Trim away any excess lining from each side of the curtain.

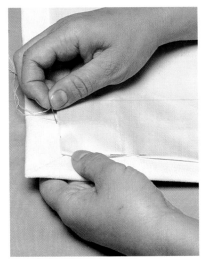

8 Turn in the edges of the lining 3 cm (1¼ in) and pin. Neatly stitch down the edges of the curtain beginning about 4 cm (1½ in) around the bottom corner and continuing until just below the heading.

9 Using a long ruler, measure from the hem of the curtain to the finished drop and mark with a pin. Repeat six times across the width of fabric. Fold fabric over to the wrong side along the marked line and pin. Finish with your chosen heading.

INTERLINED CURTAINS

Interlined curtains are more complicated to make than ordinary lined curtains, but are worth the extra time. The extra lining will provide insulation during the cold winter months, and can be used to improve the hang of more lightweight fabrics.

1 Join the widths of fabric allowed for each curtain. Press seams open, and trim away selvedges neatly.

Join widths of interlining ensuring that each width is identical to the width of the main fabric. Cut the widths to the same measurement if necessary. Join widths of lining in the same way. Press seams open.

Note: When using light-coloured fabrics, it is important that the seams of the three materials match. When light shines through the curtains, the inside seams may be visible.

2 Lay curtain fabric flat and press thoroughly to remove any creases. Lay interlining directly on top with the seams uppermost, line up the seams and hems and smooth out any wrinkles across the width. Sweep a long ruler across the fabric to help straighten the interlining in the middle of the table.

3 Turn back the interlining and lock stitch to the main fabric along each seam and twice across each width. When locking-in, always use the same colour thread as the main fabric and use large loose stitches at approximately 10 cm (4 in) intervals. Stop stitching before the top of the curtain, just below the position of the eventual headings.

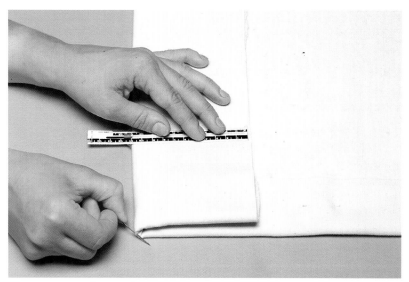

4 Reposition the interlining and smooth out any wrinkles. Turn in the main fabric and interlining 6 cm (2¼ in) down both sides of the curtain, using the measure gauge to make sure the turning is even. With your fingers, check that the interlining is well tucked into the fold to produce a firm, solid edge. Pin and press. Turn up hem 12 cm (5 in) and press.

Note: Make sure that the hemlines are equally turned and the pattern is matched for each curtain.

5 Mitre both bottom corners by firmly pressing the folded edge and hem in place and positioning a temporary pin exactly through the point of the corner.

6 Open out both folds and turn in the corner so that the pin is visible. Refold the sides and hem along the original fold lines to make the mitre, ensuring that the pin is once again on the point. With more experience you will be able to adjust the mitre so the hem and sides line up.

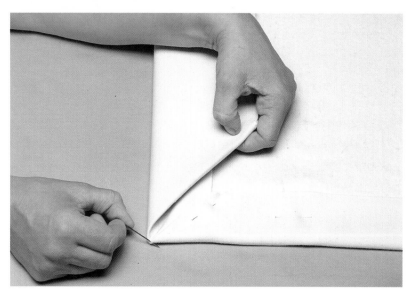

7 Open out again and cut the interlining away on the diagonal fold line that has been made. Refold the corner. Check that the pin is once again on the point and the sides and hem are straight. Pin in place and press.

8 Using stitches of approximately 5 cm (2 in), stitch down both edges, catching the back of the main fabric and both layers of interlining, but not stitching through to the front of the curtain. Using even stitches, herringbone along the hem, inserting a curtain weight into the hem at each seam. Neatly stitch up the edges of the mitre enclosing a curtain weight.

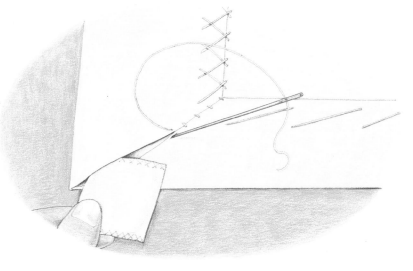

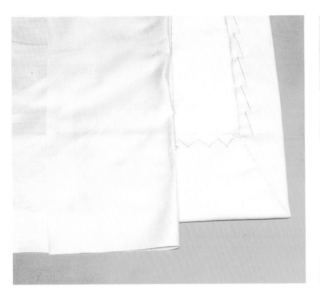

▲ **9** Carefully lay the lining on top, ensuring that it overhangs the hem of the curtain by at least 10 cm (4 in). Line up seams. Fold back the lining and starting 10 cm (4 in) above the hem, lock-in on the same lines as the interlining.

▲ **10** Ensure that the edges of the lining are level with the edges of the curtain. If not, fold back and trim.

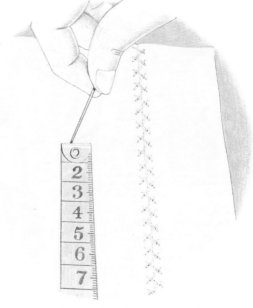

▲ **11** Turn under both edges of the lining approximately 3 cm (1¼ in) and pin. Check that the lining is not too tight as this will prevent the curtain hanging properly. Using the spare 10 cm (4 in) of lining at the bottom of the curtain, make a pocket in the lining to ease the strain if the curtain fabric drops.

▲ **12** Neatly stitch all around the lining of the curtain, remove pins and press. Measuring from the hem of the curtain, measure up to the overall drop and mark with a pin. Repeat six times across the width.

CURTAIN HEADINGS

The heading you choose will greatly determine the effect the finished curtain has on the decor of a room. Whether elaborately bunched, loosely gathered or casually tied, bear in mind the fabric weight and overall proportions of the curtains and window. When calculating curtain lengths take into account the extra fabric needed for your chosen heading.

Pleated hand headings are made using stiff buckram, generally available in widths of 10 cm (4 in) and 15 cm (6 in). If 10 cm (4 in) buckram is used, allow an extra 18 cm (7 in) to the overall drop; if using 15 cm (6 in) buckram, add 25 cm (10 in).

BUNCHED HEADING

If this heading is used on a lined or unlined curtain, more fabric will be needed to give the heading enough body. Depending on the weight of the curtains, cut a piece of net or organza, scrunch it up and fold the heading over it before stitching on the tape or, cut a piece of interlining the width of the heading allowance and place it into the heading between the main fabric and the lining before adding the tape.

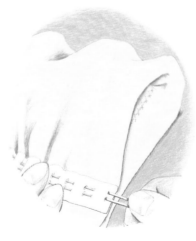

1 Measure from the marked hook drop to the end of the heading allowance and trim as necessary. Fold the lining back and trim away 3 cm (1¼ in) of the interlining. Fold the heading in half, to line up with the hook drop pin line. Pin the heading tape all along, pinning along the middle of the tape and at right angles to the tape so that the pins can remain in position while stitching. Stitch top and bottom of tape. Pull tapes and gather headings to the finished width.

2 Holding the front of the heading in one hand and the back of the heading in the other, pull both halves randomly apart and squash the heading into bunches. Pull it down over the stitching lines of the tape on the front. Sew up the open ends by hand, gathering slightly to fit in with the bunching.

3 To make a hook band, cut a piece of buckram or heading tape the width of the gathered tape and the length of the finished heading. Cut a piece of the curtain lining the same size plus 2 cm (¾ in) all around for turnings. Fold the lining over the buckram along both sides, turn in the ends and stitch.

4 Mark the curtain hooks positions with pins at 12–15 cm (5–6 in) intervals, with the overlap and return space according to the curtain fitting. The distance between the hooks will be determined by the weight of the fabric and the amount of space the curtain needs to take up when it is pulled back (the more hooks, the more space the curtain will need).

5 Pin the strip of buckram enclosed in lining along the back of the gathered heading, covering the tape completely. Stitch all along by hand.

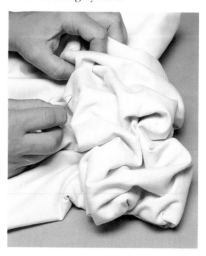

6 From the front, stab stitch randomly through the heading to hold the bunching in place. The stitching must allow the heading to remain informal – do not attempt to make the bunches too regular.

EDGED HEADING WITH TIES

To attach curtains to a pole, ties can be used in place of rings. This is especially effective for bed drapes and very lightweight curtains such as those made of silk or muslin.

1 To make up, bind the heading or turn the heading allowance over to a depth of 6–7 cm (2½–2¾ in).

2 Make ties (see Methods) to suit the size and style of curtain and fabric. Measurements between 1–2 cm (½–¾ in) wide and 25–40 cm (10–16 in) long will be ample for most curtains.

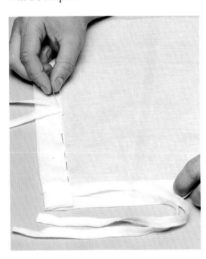

3 Insert ties two at a time into the top of the curtain heading as it is pinned in place. Fit along the width of the curtain so that the ties will be 12–15 cm (5–6 in) apart when the curtain heading is pulled up. Stitch in position, double stitching the ties to secure.

PINCH PLEATS

1 To make pinch pleats, fold back the curtain lining to the overall drop position and press lightly. If the curtain is interlined, cut away at this line. Fold the lining back up, and set the buckram onto the curtain so that the top of it lies on the pressed line, approximately 2 cm (¾ in) in from each side. Herringbone buckram in position.

2 Refold curtain over buckram and neatly tuck in edges and ends. Fold and pin pleats firmly in position at the top and bottom of the buckram. Machine stitch down the length of buckram and fasten securely.

3 To make triple French pleats, place three fingers in each pleat and flatten, then lift the pleat, pinch in the centre fold and push down to make three equal pleats.

4 At the top and base of each pleat, 2 cm (¾ in) below the buckram, stitch through the fabric to hold it in place.

GOBLETS

To make goblets, follow steps 1 and 2 for pinch pleats. Simply open out the pleat with your fingers and run a gathering thread around the base of the pleat, 1 cm (½ in) below the base of the buckram. Stuff with rolls of dacron or interlining to give a rounded shape.

GATHERED HEADING

For a gathered heading measure from the marked hook drop to the end of the heading allowance and trim away. Fold the heading allowance in half, pin the heading tape in position and stitch in place. Gather to the required width. Make up a hook band as for a bunched heading and stitch in place. Edge gathered headings with a ribbon or tape in a toning or contrasting fabric.

BINDING EDGES

The size and colour of bound edges needs to be considered carefully, so the edges are in proportion with the curtain style. Too large a binding can look very overpowering, while the colour of the binding will affect the 'impact' value of the curtain. Although there are some occasions and situations which demand strong definition and a contrast in colour, generally, edgings should be subtle, complementing the main fabric rather than competing with it.

BINDING SIDES AND HEM

In this method the binding is turned up with the hem and is used for long curtains which need the weight of the hem of the main fabric. Do not use a binding of a stronger colour than the main fabric, as it will show through.

1 Cut the binding fabric on the straight of grain and with no joins on the leading edge, the length of the curtain edges and 11 cm (4½ in) wide.

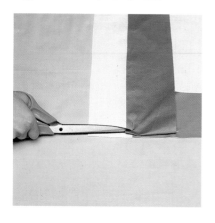

2 Place the curtain flat onto the work table, right side up. Cut away the selvedge from the leading edge. Starting at the heading, pin the edging down the length of the leading edge, matching raw edges. Position pins at right angles to the edging, to hold in place, and along the edge 1.5 cm (⅝ in) from the outside, on the stitching line. Stop pinning 9.5 cm (3¾ in) from the hem. Turn the edging and fold so that the fold line is level with the leading edge. You may snip into the corner from both sides to define the fold.

3 Stitch along the leading edge exactly 1.5 cm (⅝ in) in. It is important that the stitching line is very accurate. Stop at the corner and secure stitching. Fold the flap over and continue to stitch along the other side. The stitches should meet at the cut point, or the exact corner.

4 From the front, press the binding away from the curtain. Fold under to the back of the curtain, measuring from the front 1.5 cm (⅝ in) all along as you pin.

5 From the back, using a corner turner to give a tight point, mitre the binding.

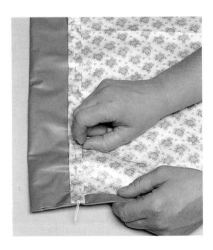

6 Herringbone stitch the binding to the curtain, taking care that the stitches are not visible on the front of the curtain.

7 Place the lining over, lock-in, turn under and stitch all around as for lined curtains. The lining should be stitched so that 1.5 cm (⅝ in) of the binding is visible on the inside all around.

BINDING UNLINED CURTAINS

This method totally encloses the raw edges on the sides and hem. No hem allowance is needed when estimating.

1 Cut the edging fabric on the straight of grain, the length of the curtain edges and 6.5 cm (2½ in) wide.

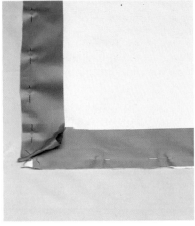

2 With the curtain face up on the work table, pin the edging strip along the leading edge, raw edges together. Pin 1.5 cm (⅝ in) in from the edge on the stitching line, with pins at right angles to anchor the fabrics while stitching. Stop pinning 1.5 cm (⅝ in) from the corner. Fold the edging so that the outside edges still line up and the fold of the edging strip lines up with the leading edge of the curtain. You may snip into this corner to identify the stitching point. Pin along the hemline.

3 Stitch along the leading edge, 1.5 cm (⅝ in) in. Stop at the snipped corner point. Secure stitches. Fold the flap over and start stitching along the other side of the point.

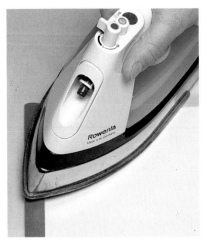

4 Press the edging strip away from the curtain, from the front. Use a damp cloth if necessary. Fold the edging under 1.5 cm (⅝ in), measuring as you pin to ensure accuracy.

5 Turn over to the back. Remove the holding pins and fold the edging strip to double under itself. Pin in place.

6 Slip stitch the edging in place and slip stitch into the machine line with small stitches to prevent any stitches showing on the front.

Right Brightly-coloured edges pick up the tones of the main curtain, and tie it visually with the small unlined curtain.

SHAPED PELMET (VALANCE)

The stiffened fabric heading for curtains which is often mounted on a wooden board or box is known as a pelmet in the UK, and a valance in the US. The box on which it is mounted is the pelmet board (or cornice).

The basic procedure for making pelmets (valances) can be used for an almost infinite variety of shapes and styles, suitable for situations from the most formal living room to a country bedroom. The length, fullness and shape of the pelmet can all be adapted using the same principles.

PREPARATION

Look at the room and consider its architectural qualities, and its use, to decide upon the pelmet (valance) shape.

Measure the width of the window and allow the stack-back for the curtains to obtain the pelmet board (cornice) size. Picture your chosen design and measure the centre depth, the highest point of any shaping and the length you wish the sides to be.

Cut a rough template from newspaper or spare wallpaper, using these measurements as your guidelines. Pin or tape the template to the pelmet board or to the wall or window frame where the board will be fitted, and mark any adjustments on the template with a pencil or pins. When you are satisfied with the template, use as the finished pattern.

Window treatments can be made attractive not only by the finishing and detailed design, but with shaped pelmet boards. A straight pelmet can look most effective when fitted to a shaped board.

The pelmet illustrated below is a simple variation on the instructions given. Simply lengthen the amount of material allowed for the lower edge to make a sweeping tail, and when gathering the fabric for the main body.

PELMET BOARDS (CORNICES)

Pelmet boards need to be made to a high standard, suiting the quality and weight of the curtaining and pelmets (valances).

For the top of the pelmet, use wood which is 2 cm (¾ in) thick, and between 12–25 cm (4–10 in) wide, depending on the proportions of the window and curtains. The sides and front should be made from plywood or medium density fibreboard (lumbercore board) 6 mm (¼ in) thick and 10–20 cm (4–8 in) deep. These will ensure that the fabric pelmet hangs straight and will not be pushed aside when the curtains are drawn.

To fix the board above the window, use cast brackets available from a specialist curtain fittings supplier. These have slots for screws, allowing some adjustment once the holes have been drilled and the screws fixed. Never use thin steel brackets as these will bend as soon as the curtains have been hung. Brackets should be placed at either end of the board, and then at 30 cm (12 in) intervals in between.

Fit the track (rod) so that the front is approximately 5 cm (2 in) from the front of the board. This measurement may vary according to the size of the curtain pleats. The heading should draw freely but not be set so far back that there is a gap between the curtains and the fabric pelmet.

MATERIALS

ruler
set square
pencil
template
cotton toile
main fabric as template
lining as template (use a contrast lining if it will show)
domette or lightweight interlining as template
velcro – the length of the finished width
heading tapes as chosen

1 Using a metal ruler and set square mark one half of the template into divisions. Use approximately 4–5 cm (2 in) spacing where there is little shaping and 2–3 cm (1–1½ in) spacing where there is more shaping. Number these divisions starting at the centre.

2 Place the cotton toile onto the work table. Cut half the pelmet pattern along the marked lines. Starting at the centre and working outwards, place the paper strips onto the toile, leaving gaps the width of each strip to make the fullness. If a fuller gather is required, leave more space between strips.

Line up the tops of the strips against a straight edge. Add the return of the pelmet board and equivalent fullness to either side of the main fabric.

3 When all pieces are in place, cut around the lower edge following the lowest point of each piece. Check that the line runs smoothly. Fold the fabric in half and repeat with the other side.

4 Run a large gathering thread through the fabric approximately 4 cm (1¾ in) from the top. Gather up to the template size. Fit against the window to check the shaping and make any adjustments.

5 Use the cotton toile as a guide to cut the main fabric, lining and interlining, joining widths as necessary and adding seam allowances of 2.5 cm (1 in). Place interlining over main fabric, locking into position as for interlined curtains, and snipping into any curves along the hem to ensure the fabric lies flat.

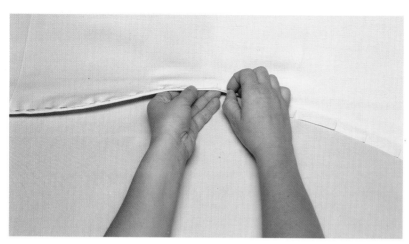

6 Place lining over the interlining and lock-in on seams and along the same lines as the interlining lock stitches. Trim the lining along the hemline so that 1 cm (½ in) overhangs the pelmet edge. Turn under 1.5 cm (⅝ in) and pin all along. Slip stitch in place. Pin fabrics together along the top.

7 Using the long side of the ruler, mark a straight line and tidy up the top edge if necessary. Measure from the top and turn over the allocated heading allowance. (If the interlining is bulky, fold the lining back along the fold line and trim the interlining away.) Pin on the heading tape and stitch top and bottom from the same direction to prevent the fabric pulling. Turn to the front and stitch braid, fringe or other trimming along the hemline.

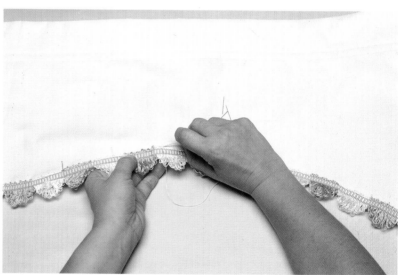

8 Gather the pelmet up to the finished width. Cut a long piece of lining fabric to the finished width of the pelmet plus 3 cm (1¼ in). Stitch the velcro along the centre of this piece. Press both sides of the lining under, leaving enough at each side of the velcro to stitch into. Pin this strip to the back of the heading tape. Turn under the raw edges at each end and stitch in place. Cords or ropes may be stitched along the top edge if desired.

SIMPLE SWAG AND TAIL

Swags and tails are the most elegant of window treatments. To look their best they need to dress tall windows with elegant proportions, and are best suited to period rooms. The swag described here is simpler to make up than the traditional draped swag, but its pleated effect is no less effective. It is important to balance the depth of the swag with the length of the tails when calculating the amount of fabric that will be required.

To calculate the amount of fabric needed, measure the length of the pelmet board (cornice) without the return measurements and the depth of the centre of the shaping. The piece of fabric for each swag will be the finished width plus 16 cm (6½ in) and the finished length times three.

MATERIALS

main fabric
lining
mediumweight interlining
heavy-duty thread to match main fabric
heading tape the length of the swag
canvas for toile

1 Cut the main fabric to the size estimated and place this on the table face down. Cut the two sides so that the swag tapers from top to bottom by 5 cm (2 in) on each side, reducing the top to the finished width plus 6 cm (2½ in).

2 To shape the lower edge slightly, start cutting 8 cm (3 in) up from each side and curving down towards the centre of the swag.

3 Cut the other swags, the lining and the mediumweight interlining to the same pattern.

4 Place the swag face down, place the interlining over and lock stitch at 30 cm (12 in) intervals across the width. Trim the interlining away 2 cm (¾ in) inside the main fabric, and herringbone along the hemline to secure. Turn up the hemline and herringbone to the interlining. Fold over both sides 3 cm (1¼ in) and pin in place.

5 Place the lining over the interlining and lock together. Pin fabrics together along the top. Score the lining along the curved lower edge and trim back to 0.5 cm (¼ in). Turn under 1.5 cm (⅝ in), pin to hold, and slip stitch.

6 Thread two large needles with doubled heavy-duty cotton to match the main fabric. The threads should be about 60 cm (24 in) long.

Secure one needle 1 cm (½ in) from the edge, inside the lining, and the other 3 cm (1¼ in) from the edge. Stitch running stitches of 1.5 cm (⅝ in) from the bottom to the top, gathering slightly to prevent the need for extra thread.

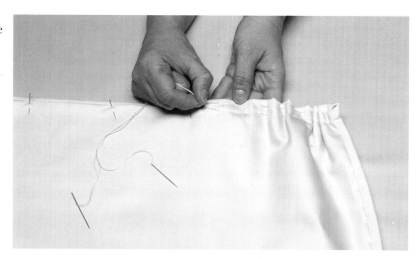

7 At the top, pull both threads together, tight enough to take up all of the slack. Check that the depth of the centre of the pelmet board (cornice) and the swag depth are as required, and adjust if necessary. Knot to secure, and double stitch into the fabric.

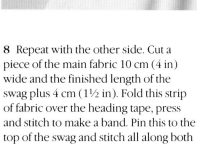

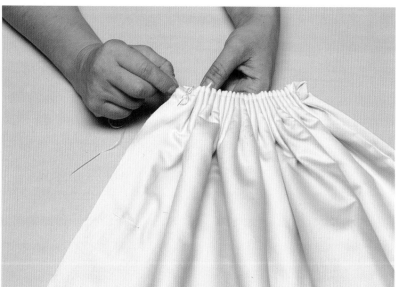

8 Repeat with the other side. Cut a piece of the main fabric 10 cm (4 in) wide and the finished length of the swag plus 4 cm (1½ in). Fold this strip of fabric over the heading tape, press and stitch to make a band. Pin this to the top of the swag and stitch all along both sides to join.

9 Using the examples as a guide, cut a canvas toile to establish the drape of the tail. Tack (baste) interlining to the back to give the pattern a realistic weight, fold the toile and stitch the pleats firmly in place. Pin to the pelmet board and adjust as necessary.

10 When you are happy with the result, use the toile to cut around the main fabric, allowing 1 cm (½ in) seam allowance on the sides and 6 cm (2½ in) for the heading. Use tacking to mark any folds. Cut a second tail, reversing all shaping, and cut lining and interlining to the same pattern.

11 Place interlining over main fabric and lock in place. If using heavy interlining cut the interlining 1 cm (½ in) away from the insides of the tail. Herringbone to the main fabric, turn in main fabric 1 cm (½ in) and pin.

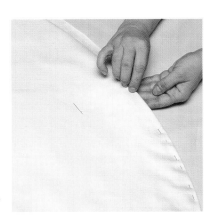

12 Place the lining over the interlining and lock together. Pin the lining to the edge of the tail on the shaped sides, and 1 cm (½ in) from the edge on the end, and stitch in place. Do not stitch the lining to the top of the tail.

13 Fold back the lining from the top, cut away 6 cm (2½ in) of interlining, leaving the side return and 12 cm (5 in) at the inside edge untrimmed. Herringbone securely to the main fabric.

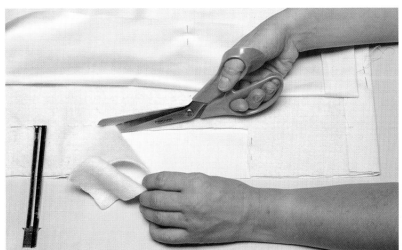

14 Pleat the heading to the required size following the markings and measurements on the toile.

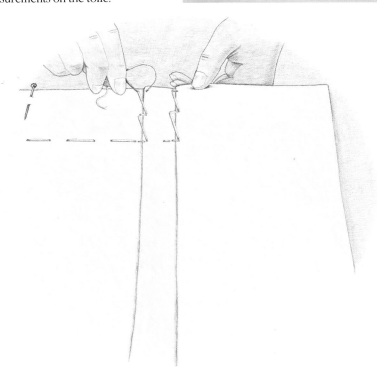

15 Pin heading tape across the top, 1 cm (½ in) inside the seam allowance, and tack in place.

16 Test the tail on the pelmet board to check that it hangs well, and adjust if necessary. Unpick the tape and cover with main fabric. To finish, use thumb size drawing pins (thumb tacks) to fix swags and tail to the board, and make a rosette, choux or cross to cover the centre join (see Accessories).

TIE-BACKS

Tie-backs should be as practical as they are decorative, with the drape and fullness of the curtain fabric dictating whether a tie-back is necessary. Small window treatments and light, unlined curtains may look overly fussy if there is scant material to warrant being pulled away from the window. If the material hangs straight, the tie-back will look little more than a fabric 'belt'.

To calculate the size and shape of the tie-back, hold a piece of fabric around the curtain and pin together at the back, adjusting the width and length until the curtain drapes well. When you are satisfied with the result, use this as a template.

MATERIALS

calico template
main fabric
heavy pelmet (valance) buckram or two
    layers of curtain heading buckram
heavy interlining
piping (cord)
edgings (optional)
1 × 2 cm (¾ in) brass ring

SHAPED AND PIPED (CORDED) TIE-BACKS

Shaped tie-backs provide a tailored look to window treatments, but need not be any less decorative. Unusual shapes, contrasting edgings, bindings or cords, and bows or rosettes as finishing touches will create interesting – and individual – treatments. If the window is dressed for effect rather than function, creases in the main fabric will not matter, so a very tight tie-back can be used to give a full 'bunched' look to the curtain.

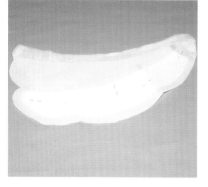

1 Use the template to cut pieces from the main fabric, adding a seam allowance of 1.5 cm (⅝ in) all around. You will need to cut two pieces for each tie-back. Cut one piece of heavy interlining and one piece of pelmet buckram or two pieces of heading buckram to the template size. Pin the piece of interlining to the wrong side of the tie-back front piece.

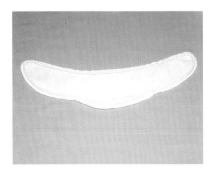

▲ **2** Pin the piping (cord) all around the tie-back front piece, along the seam allowance. Join the ends of the cord at the end of the tie-back which will be behind the curtain.

3 Stitch the piping in place. Place this piece face down on the work table and press in the seam allowance. If the fabric is bulky, trim the interlining back to the stitching line. Snip into the seam allowance to make sure the piping lies flat and fit the buckram under the pressed-in seam allowance, against the interlining.

4 Trim away half the seam allowance on the back piece and pin to the piping at the centre top, bottom and both ends. Fold under the seam allowance and pin to the remaining sections of piping.

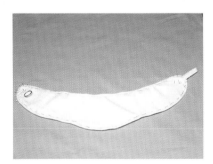

▲ **5** Make a loop from a piece of the main fabric and pin to the end of the tie-back which will be behind the curtain. Stitch the brass ring to the other end and slip stitch all round.

BOWS

Large bows and sashes are very effective in feminine room treatments. They are practical as tie-backs for curtains, and may be used to tie cushion covers, or to decorate headboards, pelmets (valances), and dressing tables.

1 Allow four pieces of fabric for each tie-back; cut to the length and width required, plus 2 cm (¾ in) seam allowances, with the ends approximately double the width of the sash. Pin the pieces together along the sides and across one end, and stitch all around the pinned sides. Trim the seam allowance to 1 cm (½ in) and the corners away to within 3 mm (⅛ in) of the stitching.

2 Turn inside out through the narrow end, pulling the corners out with a pin to give neat points.

▲ **3** Press ties flat, fold both ends in and pleat to approx 4 cm (1½ in). Stitch brass rings to each end.

4 Fit both ends onto the tie-back hook and tie bows at the front or side of the curtain. These bows may be stitched in place as the tie-backs will be operated from the rings.

PLAITED TIE-BACK

Use three strips of material 12 cm (5 in) wide and twice the length of the finished tie-back. Fill each strip with rolled pieces of dacron or interlining, plait (braid) together, and finish with a brass ring as for the shaped tie-back. Decorate with a rosette, choux, cross or bow (see Accessories).

ACCESSORIES

The following accessories can be used to embellish tie-backs, sewn onto curtain drapes, or attached to cushion covers or headboards – experiment with different weights and textures of fabric for different effects.

SIMPLE ROSES

The following instructions can be used to create full-blown roses or small 'buds'. Use a fabric that will gather tightly without creasing.

△ **1** Cut fabric strips, fold in half lengthways, and cut along the raw edges so that one end is wider than the other. Run a gathering thread along the raw edges, stitching with double thread through both layers.

◁ **2** Pull the gathering thread up so that the strip is approximately half its original length. Starting from the narrow end, make a centre and gradually wind the rest of the fabric around, gathering more as you go along, as tightly as you wish the finished rose to be. Hold the raw edges together and wind the thread around the ends, approximately 1 cm (½ in) in. Finish with a small piece of fabric to enclose the raw edges.

CHOUX

Choux in any size can be added as a decorative finish to pelmets (valances) and tie-backs.

1 Cut a square of fabric to the required size: 45 cm (18 in) will make a 10 cm (4 in) choux rosette.

2 Stitch a running stitch with double thread all around, 1.5 cm (⅝ in) in from the raw edge. Pull up and secure in the centre.

3 Cut a 6 cm (2½ in) square of buckram, a 9 cm (3½ in) square of the fabric and a 10 cm (4 in) piece of narrow curtain heading tape. Cover the buckram with the fabric and stitch in the centre. Stitch the end of the tape to the middle of the fabric and buckram. Press in the raw edges to make a 6 cm (2½ in) square. Stitch all around the gathers to enclose raw edges.

4 Place the choux flat on the table and pull up the gathers from the front. Cup both sides of the fabric in both hands and use your fingers to make crevices and peaks until you are happy with the shape of the choux. Using double thread stitch through the choux at random, starting by stitching around the outside and pulling the choux into the diameter chosen. Do not stitch too tightly or you will end with a flat, uninteresting shape.

CROSSES

Use crosses to decorate pelmets (valances), or swags and tails. They can also be used with ropes and cords, as a striking addition to a formal window treatment.

1 Cut two pieces of fabric the length and width of the chosen bow size plus 1.5 cm (⅝ in) all around for the seam allowances. Fold in half with the right sides inside. Stitch along the short edges, leaving a 5 cm (2 in) gap in the middle. Press seams flat and refold each bow so that the seam runs along the centre back.

2 Trim seams and cut across the corners to within 3 mm (⅛ in) of the stitching line. Turn right side out and use a pin to pull the corners into a square. Press seams.

3 Using double thread, stitch either side of the centre. Pull up and secure. Repeat with the other bow.

4 Place one bow on top of the other, stitch together, and finish with a button (see below) or other decorative feature.

5 To make buttons, cut a circle of buckram to the finished diameter. Cut two pieces of dacron and one piece of interlining to this size. Cut one circle of main fabric three times this diameter. Using double thread and tiny stitches, stitch a gathering thread all around. Place the dacron, interlining and buckram in this order into the centre of the circle. Pull the gathering thread up and secure.

BLINDS (SHADES)

 Blinds are both practical and stylish window treatments, that can be used in conjunction with curtains or as an alternative to curtains in an awkwardly placed window. The clean, spare lines of Roman and roller blinds are particularly suited to small windows in kitchens and bathrooms, while the elaborate look of Austrian blinds will provide sumptuous decoration in a period room treatment.

Below *To make a cascade blind, add approximately 3 cm (1¼ in) to the overall width of the window for each scallop, and make up as for Roman blinds, without the rods. Make a pleat in the heading at each gather to absorb the fullness.*

ROMAN BLIND (SHADE)

Roman blinds will give a clean, uncluttered look to windows, and can be used when there is little room for curtain stack-back, or where an obstruction, such as a radiator, makes full length curtains impossible.

Choose a good quality, firm fabric which will not pucker when sewn, and avoid large patterns and those which will look unbalanced when the blind is folded up. Stripes may be difficult to make up, whereas checks look fresh and give good stitching guidance. Remember that geometric patterns are woven on the straight of grain.

MATERIALS

main fabric
lining
lightweight interlining (optional)
pencil or vanishing marker
ruler
set square
velcro (twin) the width of the finished blind
1.25 cm (½ in) wooden dowels cut to 3 cm (1¼ in) less than the finished blind width
2.5 cm (1 in) solid brass rings
2.5 cm (1 in) lath cut 2 cm (¾ in) less than the finished blind width
blind (shade) cord
1 batten 5 cm × 2.5 cm (2 in × 1 in), the width of the finished blind
screw eyes
1 cleat
1 cord weight

CALCULATING FABRIC

1 Decide whether the blind is to fit inside or outside the window frame or reveal. Measure the width and length at 20 cm (8 in) intervals. Allow 10 cm (4 in) for hems and headings and 12 cm (5 in) for side turnings.

   Note: A Roman blind (shade) should never be more than 220 cm (88 in) wide. The rods will start to bend and the blind (shade) will not pull up evenly beyond this width.

2 To find the amount of fabric needed,
   a) divide the measured width plus side turnings by the width of your fabric.
   example Finished width
   150 cm + 12 cm = 162 cm ÷ 135 cm = 1.1 widths
   (60 in + 5 in = 65 in ÷ 54 in = 1.1 widths)
   Round up to the next width of fabric.
   b) Multiply the widths by the finished length of the blind plus hem and heading allowance.
   example Finished length
   200 cm + 10 cm × 2 = 420 cm
   (80 in + 4 in × 2 = 168 in)
   420 cm (168 in) of fabric is needed.

3 You will now need to determine the size of the folds. Aim to make a blind which will take up approximately 17–19 cm (7–8 in) of space when folded up. Rods will be stitched at the top of each fold, with 30–35 cm (12–14 in) between each. The lowest fold should be half as long as the others, plus 2.5 cm (1 in).
   a) Take the finished drop of the blind (shade) and deduct 2 cm (¾ in). Divide the rest by approximately 15 cm (6 in).
   example Finished blind
   116 cm − 2 cm = 114 cm ÷ 15 = 7.60
   (46 in − ¾ in = 45¼ in ÷ 6 = 7.54)
   b) Divide the length by the nearest uneven number:
   114 cm ÷ 7 = 16.29 cm
   (45¼ in ÷ 7 = 6½ in)
   The lower blind fold will be:
   16.29 cm + 2 cm (6½ in + ¾ in) and the other sections will be 32.58 cm (13 in). Round up or down if necessary.

1 Join the widths of fabric as necessary, sewing half a width either side of the centre panel, to avoid a centre seam.

2 Cut the lining to allow rod pockets of 5.5 cm (2 ¼ in), hem and heading allowances of 10 cm (4 in), and side turning allowances of 6 cm (2½ in). If using interlining, cut to the same measurements as the main fabric.

3 Join the lining and interlining widths so that the seams line up with the main fabric. Press the lining sides 3 cm (1¼ in) to the wrong side and pin in place.

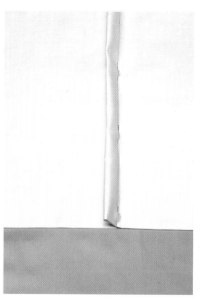

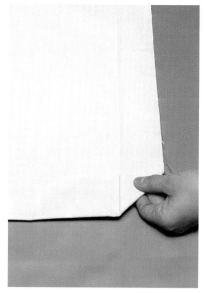

▲ 4 Cut the hemline of the lining straight, using the set square for accuracy.

▲ 5 Using a soft pencil or vanishing marker measure up from the hemline and mark the stitching lines for the rod pockets.
Note: These measurements must be exact or the blind will not fold up straight. All measurements must be taken from the bottom line and not from the previous mark, to avoid error.
Pin the folds and stitch in place, keeping the sides even and stitching from one direction to prevent the fabric pulling.

▲ 6 Place the main fabric face down onto the work table. Turn in the sides 6 cm (2½ in) and herringbone in place. Turn up the hem allowance and mitre over the bottom corner.

▲ 7 Place the lining over the main fabric, pockets outwards. Carefully line up seams and hemline, and pin the sides securely. Pin each of the pocket stitching lines with pins at right angles to the stitching, and pockets facing upwards.

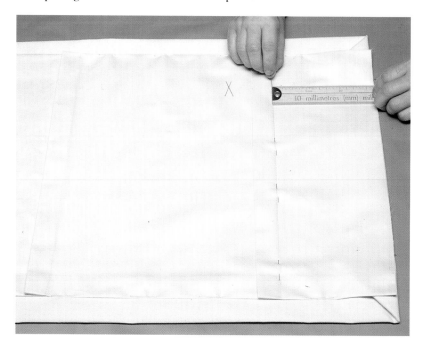

8 Machine stitch along the pocket lines, stitching from one direction to avoid fabric pulling to one side. Measuring from the hem upwards, at 30 cm (12 in) intervals across the blind, mark the finished length. Turn to the wrong side and press. Trim to 2 cm (¾ in) more than the finished length, pin the velcro strip to cover the raw edge, and stitch in place.

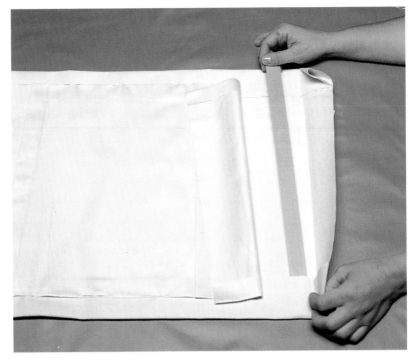

9 With the blind face down on the table again, insert one rod into each pocket and stitch each end of the pocket to close. Insert the lath into the bottom of the blind through the mitred corners.

10 Slip stitch the lining to the main fabric. Mark the ring positions, starting 5–8 cm (2–3 in) in from each side. Stitch rings thoroughly in place to the top of the rod pockets.

11 Tie the end of the length of cord into the lowest ring and stitch to secure. Pass up through the row, along the top and down the side to the bottom corner. Repeat with the other cords, until they are all at the same point.

12 Cover the batten with the main fabric, staple velcro onto the top and fit the batten to the blinds. Fix screw eyes into the batten in line with the rows of cords and attach a cord carrier to the cord ends.

13 Fix the batten in position and screw the cleat to the window frame or wall. Raise and lower the blind several times to ensure that the cords are free and straight. Fit the cord weight and knot cords at the cleat level, and cut away excess cords.

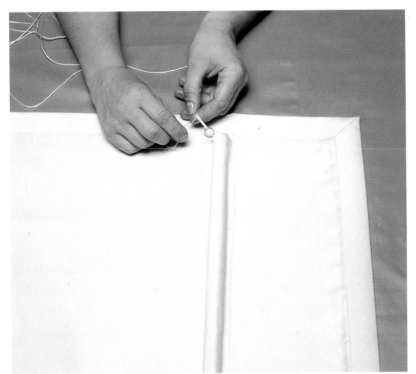

AUSTRIAN BLIND (SHADE)

Austrian blinds are those which look like curtains when down, with the fullness of the fabric across the width. The lower edge is often trimmed with a frill, fringe or contrast binding. If the blind is to be used for decoration and fitted in front of the window recess, a frilled edging may be added to both sides. Austrian blinds are made longer than the space to be covered, with the lower edge gathered up to form scallops.

Care needs to be taken in estimating the fullness of fabric needed. Blinds which are too full will be untidy — instead of looking attractive they may give the impression that the fabric has been pulled up and stored on top of the window simply because no one knew what else to do with it.

Decide on the length of the finished blind and allow approximately 30 cm (12 in) for the fabric to make scallops, and 10 cm (4 in) each for the heading and hem allowance. If the blind is to fall to the floor it usually looks best hanging as a curtain, so the extra length needed to make the scallops will not be necessary.

MATERIALS

main fabric
lining
interlining (optional)
pencil or vanishing marker
ruler
1.25 cm (½ in) solid brass rings (clear plastic rings can be used but will become brittle and yellow with washing and sunlight)
Austrian blind cord
heading tape (pencil pleat or gathering)
velcro (twin) the length of the batten plus returns
1 batten 5 cm × 2.5 cm (2 in × 1 in), the width of the finished blind
stapler
screw eyes
1 cord carrier
1 cord weight
1 cleat

CALCULATING FABRIC

1 Calculate the number of widths of fabric required by multiplying the finished width of the blind (shade) by 1.5 to 2.5 depending on the fullness required.
example Finished width
110 cm × 2 = 220 cm
(44 in × 2 = 88 in)

2 Divide this figure by the width of your fabric.
example
220 ÷ 135 = 1.63
(88 ÷ 54 = 1.63)

3 Round up to the next width of fabric. If your calculation shows that you need just over a full width you might decide to allow slightly less fullness, to prevent wastage of spare fabric, or you might want to increase the fullness to take up more of the 'spare' fabric.

4 Calculate the cut lengths needed by adding the scallop, hem and heading allowances to the required finished length.
example Finished length
150 cm + 10 cm (heading) + 10 cm (hem) + 30 cm (scallop)
(60 in + 4 in (heading) + 4 in (hem) + 12 in (scallop)).

5 If the fabric is patterned calculate the cut length needed by dividing the finished drop by the pattern repeat.
Allow up to the next complete repeat.

6 Multiply this cut by the number of fabric widths required.

1 Join the widths of fabric if necessary, sewing half a width to either side of a full width to avoid a centre seam. Cut and join the lining and interlining in the same manner. Press seams open, trimming away selvedges and any selvedge writing.

Note: Seams must be trimmed evenly as any jagged edges will be very obvious once light shines through the hanging blind.

2 Place the fabric face down onto the work table and place interlining on top, matching all seams. Lock stitch the interlining to the main fabric on the seams and at 30 cm (12 in) intervals across each width. Turn in the sides 10 cm (4 in) and pin in place. Turn the hem up 10 cm (4 in) and put a pin into the corner point which has now been made. Open out the hem fold. Fold the hem corner over onto the side, turning at a 45° angle and pin to hold.

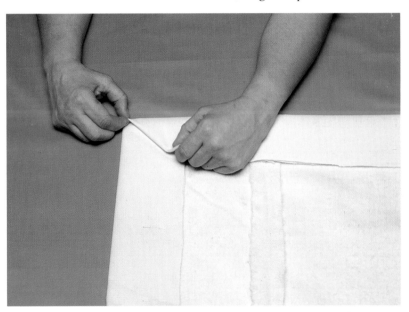

3 Trim the interlining seam back to 3 mm (⅛ in) up to the hem fold line. Fold the hem line back on the first fold line and make a false mitre.

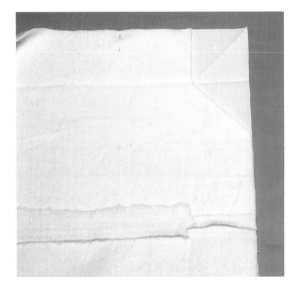

4 If the interlining and fabric are both bulky, open up the fold again and cut the interlining away at the corner along the fold lines so that the corners lie flat.

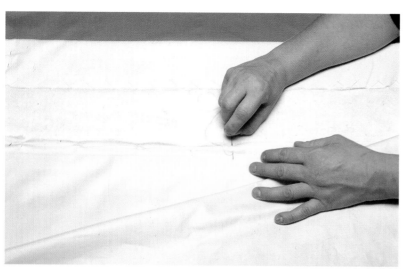

5 Stitch all around the blind with herringbone stitches approximately 2 cm (¾ in) apart.

◄ **6** Place the lining onto the main fabric, matching seams carefully. Lock stitch the lining to the main fabric or to the interlining on the seams and at 30 cm (12 in) intervals across the width.

▼ **7** Smooth the lining over the sides of the main fabric. Fold back so that 7 cm (2¾ in) of the main fabric is visible on both sides and along the hem, and trim away excess lining.

8 Turn the lining in 1.5 cm (⅝ in) all around. Pin and slip stitch in place. (Approximately 8.5 cm/3¾ in of main fabric will now be visible all around the lining.) Remove pins and press lightly.

9 Measure up from the hem to the finished drop, at 30 cm (12 in) intervals across the blind, and mark with pins. Fold the fabric and lining over to the lining side. Press lightly and pin in place. If you have used interlining, fold back the lining, and cut the interlining away along the fold line. Pin to hold.

10 Mark the ring positions with crossed pins. Always measure each ring position from the bottom to avoid error. The outside rows should be on the lining edge, and there should be a row at each seam to produce two to three scallops per width.

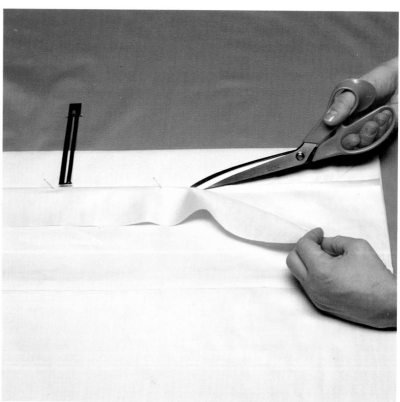

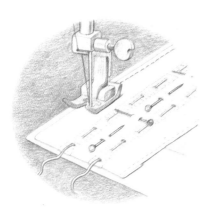

◄ **11** Trim heading allowance to suit your chosen heading tape. Pin the tape in position at 10 cm (4 in) intervals along the centre of the tape with the heads facing away from the machine foot, and vertical pins at 10 cm (4 in) intervals in between. Stitch along the top and bottom edges leaving the pins in place to prevent the fabric pulling.

If you want to make an invisible heading, pin the heading tape to the right side of the blind. Pin across the tape and along the centre of the tape as above. The pins will stay in position while stitching to keep the fabric from pulling. Stitch along the top edge only.

12 Turn the tape to the wrong side and pin as before. Hand sew the lower edge of the tape to the blind. This will prevent a ridge of machine stitching sinking into the fabrics. Pull up to the finished blind width plus the returns (2.5 cm/1 in each side of the batten).

13 Cut a piece of lining 6 cm (2½ in) wide and the length of the finished heading. Stitch the strip of velcro to the centre of this piece. Press both sides under, leaving the strip 3 cm (1¼ in) wide. Stitch across the heading tape to enclose the tape completely.

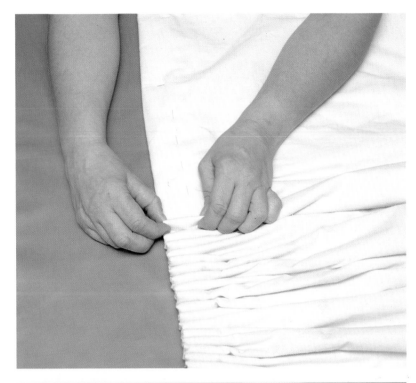

14 Stitch each ring thoroughly in position by stitching into the lining three or four times, then stitch through into the main fabric once, and twice more into the lining. Twist the cotton around the stitched threads several times. Fasten off with a double stitch into the threads.

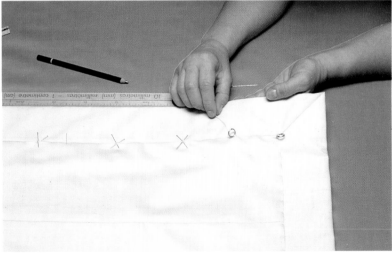

15 Tie one end of the cord to the bottom ring on the right hand side. Stitch the cords together for approximately 5 cm (2 in) to strengthen, avoiding an ugly knot which could easily pull out. Thread the cord up the blind through each ring, run it along the top of the blind and down the left hand side. Cut off at the hemline and repeat with the other cords, so that all cords finish at the same point.

16 Cover the batten with the main fabric. Staple the other side of the velcro to the front and sides. Fix to the velcro on the blind. Fit screw eyes into the batten at the top of each row and a cord carrier to the cord ends.

Fit the batten in position and screw the cleat to the window frame or wall. Thread each cord through the screw eyes starting at the side with one cord. Work along the blind, passing each cord through the screw eye in line with each row of rings and through all other screw eyes towards the end of the batten until all cords are through the carrier.

Holding all cords together firmly, pull the blind up and down several times. Look behind the blind to check that cords are not twisted or caught up. Cut cords evenly. Thread through the cord weight and knot securely to make sure that the cords cannot pull through.

CUSHIONS

 Mounds of cushions may be heaped onto a favourite sofa or armchair to create an irresistibly inviting atmosphere and provide an instant lift to any room scheme. Use scatter cushions to provide accents of colour, to pick up colour details in the curtains or upholstery, or to display unusual or cherished pieces of fabric such as tapestry, embroidery or old lace. The following pages explain how to make basic cushions and edgings, so mix fabrics and embellish liberally for a sumptuous display.

Below Cushions provide a quick and easy way to define a room scheme. Here, bright Provençal prints combine perfectly with iron furniture.

BASIC PIPED (CORDED) CUSHION

```
MATERIALS

main fabric
piping (cord)
zip
cushion pad
```

CALCULATING FABRIC

1 Allow 1.5 cm (5/8 in) seam allowance for the cushion front.
2 Cut two pieces for the back to allow the zip to be fitted. The main piece should have a 2 cm (3/4 in) seam allowance on the lower edge for the zip, and a 1.5 cm (5/8 in) seam allowance on the other three sides. Cut a bottom strip 5 cm (2 in) wide, plus the 2 cm (3/4 in) zip allowance and 1.5 cm (5/8 in) seam allowance.

1 Make up the piping (cord). Place the front and two back pieces together on the work table, right sides facing and notch at least once on all sides.

2 On the front piece, starting from the bottom of the cushion, pin the piping all around on the seam allowance. Stop 1.5 cm (5/8 in) from each corner. Snip right into the piping stitching line, and position so that the cut is now at a 90° angle and the corner is 'square'.

3 Join the piping (see Methods) and stitch the zip between the two back pieces.

4 Matching the notches, pin the back of the cushion to the front. Pin along the seam line and at right angles to it so that these pins may remain in position whilst stitching, to prevent the fabric moving.

5 Stitch all around as close to the piping stitching line as possible. Turn to the front and if the previous stitches are visible, re-stitch inside the last line. Cut away the corner to within 3 mm (1/8 in) of the stitching line, and stitch across the corners to secure. Turn right side out, pushing the corners out to a neat square with the point of your scissors.

Fill with the cushion pad, plumping well to make sure that the corners have enough filling. ▶

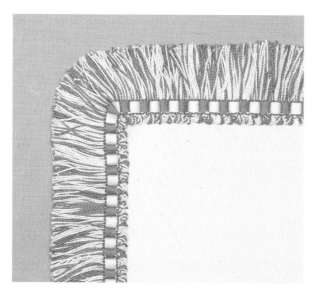

STITCHED ON TRIMMING

Make up as basic cushion without the piping (cord) and press. Pin the trimming all around, stitching along the inside edge of the trimming and along the edge of the cushion cover.

CORD WITH KNOTTED CORNERS

Make up as basic cushion without the piping (cord) and press. Stitch cord all around with small stitches, weaving into the cord and through the edge of the cushion cover so that stitches are invisible. Knot each corner and stitch.

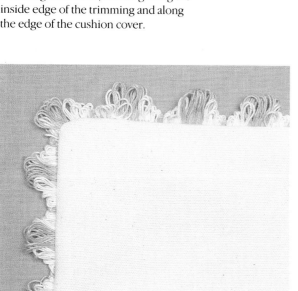

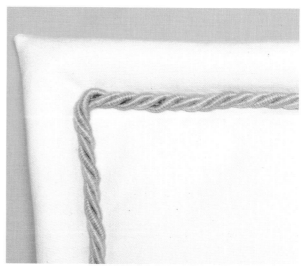

INSET FAN EDGING

Make up as basic cushion, using the fan edge instead of the piping (cord).

ROLLED EDGE

Make up as basic cushion without the piping (cord). Make four rolls of interlining to fit inside the cushion edge. Stitch around inside by hand. Stitch cord all around, on top of stitching line. The cord can be stitched inside the roll on the back to make the cushion reversible, as it will cover the zip opening.

OXFORD-STYLE CUSHION

Oxford-style cushions are characterized by their crisp, tailored corners. The steps below are for a true Oxford, but a similar effect can be achieved with a 'false' Oxford. Simply make up a basic cushion (see p 61) without the piping (cord), adding 10–12cm (4–5in) all around for the flap. Turn right side out, press and satin stitch all around, 5–6cm (2–3in) from the outside edge.

CALCULATING FABRIC

1 For the front piece, add 25 cm (10 in) to the dimensions of the cushion pad (ie, a 45 cm/18 in pad will need a piece cut 70 cm/28 in square).
2 Cut the back piece to the same width as the front, adding 5 cm (2 in) to the length for the zip.

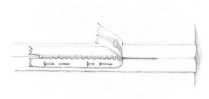

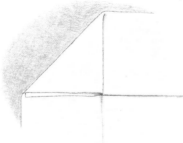

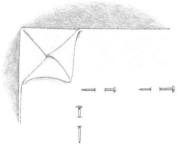

1 Cut 14 cm (5½ in) from the back length. Pin back to the same place, taking 2.5 cm (1 in) allowance for the zip. Stitch 14 cm (5½ in) in from each side. Press. Insert the zip.

2 Place both pieces on the work table, with the right sides down. Working with each side consecutively, fold and press over 7 cm (2¾ in). Fold the corners under in turn, to make a false mitre. Pin in place.

3 Place the pieces wrong sides together. Line up so that each corner is folded in the opposite way, so that the corners lie flat and meet each other. Pin all around, 5 cm (2 in) in from the edge.

4 Satin stitch all around following the pinned line. The flaps should be free, but firmly stitched along this line. Open up the zip and fill with the cushion pad.

PIPED AND FRILLED CUSHION

There is endless scope for variations on the basic cover described below. Use a patterned cover for the main fabric, with another pattern for the edging and piping (cord). Or use bound rope in a suitable colour instead of the piping on the inside of the frill. You could make a double frill, with the frills in contrasting colours to display your favourite fabrics, allowing 1.5 cm (⅝ in) difference between the width of each frill.

CALCULATING FABRIC

1 Allow 2.5 cm (1 in) seam allowance all around for the front cover.
2 Add 5 cm (2 in) to the back length to allow for the zip.
3 For a plain frill of double fullness, cut a strip of fabric twice as long as the overall dimensions of the cushion pad, the width desired plus seam allowances.
4 For a bound frill, cut two strips the length as above, with one strip 2.5 cm (1 in) narrower in width.

MATERIALS

main fabric
fabric for frills
piping (cord)
zip
cushion pad

1 Insert the zip into back cover.

2 Make the frills. For a plain frill, press fabric in half lengthways and join the short ends to form a loop. Stitch a gathering thread 1.5 cm (⅝ in) in from the raw edge.

For bound frills, stitch the pieces together along the length, with a 1.5 cm (⅝ in) seam allowance. This seam allowance must be stitched accurately. Press the fabrics from the right side, pressing towards the binding fabric. Fold under so that 1.5 cm (⅝ in) of the binding remains visible on the front. Pin all around. Stitch the short ends together to make a loop and press seams flat. Stitch a gathering thread all around, 1.5 cm (⅝ in) in from the raw edge.

3 Measure the frill length. Divide by 8 and mark with tacks (basting stitches) in a contrasting thread.

4 Pin piping (cord) to the front piece of the cushion. Join and stitch in the same way as the basic cushion (see p 61). Mark halfway along each side with tacks in a contrasting thread.

5 Gather the frill slightly. Using the tacks as markers, pin the frill to the cushion front and pull up gathers evenly between these points. Pin along and across the piping line. Stitch, leaving the pins across the piping.

6 Turn over and check that the piping stitching line is not visible. If it is, re-stitch inside the previous line.

7 Open the zip up slightly. Pin the back to the front, matching corners and notches. Stitch in close to the piping line as before. Keep stitching in closely to cover any previous stitching, and to keep the piping tight. Press and fill with the pad.

BUTTERFLY FRILL CUSHION

A variation on the simple frill, the butterfly frill is suitable for feminine room treatments. Here a glazed cotton fabric was used, ensuring a crisp, fresh result.

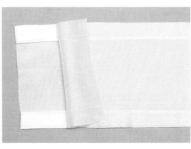

1 Pin piping along both lengths of one of the frill pieces, 1.5 cm (⅝ in) in from the raw edges. Stitch in place.

2 Pin the other frill on top and stitch close to the piping line.

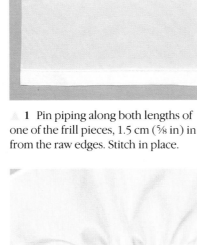

3 Turn right side out and press along the piping line. Stitch a gathering thread approximately 2.5–3 cm (1–1¼ in) in from the edge.

MATERIALS

main fabric
fabric for frills
narrow piping (cord) for frills
zip
cushion pad

CALCULATING FABRIC

1 Allow 2.5 cm (1 in) seam allowance all around for the front cover.
2 Add 5 cm (2 in) to the back length to allow for the zip.
3 For the frills, cut 2 strips 13 cm (5 in) wide, twice the length of the overall cushion dimensions.

4 Stitch the two short ends together, lining up the piping and seams. Divide the length of the frill by 8 and mark with tacks (basting stitches) at these intervals. Stitch a tack to the cushion front halfway along each side. Pin the frill to the cushion front with the gathering line 6 cm (2½ in) in from the edge. Match the tacks on the frill to the cushion corners and the tacks along the sides. Stitch with zigzag stitches, and remove gathering threads.

5 Join the back, with a 2.5 cm (1 in) seam allowance, for 5 cm (2 in) along each side. Stitch the zip into the opening. Open up and pin the cushion back to the cushion front, avoiding the frill. Stitch all around and neaten the seam. Turn right side out and fill with the pad. Plump up to make sure that the corners are well filled.

BOX CUSHION

A box cushion is simply one with a gusset between the top and bottom pieces, thus creating a 'boxed' shape. Box cushions are mainly used as seat cushions for occasional chairs, armchairs and sofas, but if they are small enough they can be used as decorative scatter cushions on side chairs or large sofas.

Fillings range from the luxurious and long-lasting duck or goosedown to a mixture of down and feather, or, for a firmer cushion, foam. All fillings are available in a variety of price ranges. Always overstuff cushions initially to make up for the flattening that will occur with use.

MATERIALS

main fabric
piping (cord)
zip, the width of the cushion plus 15 cm
    (6 in) either side
cushion pad

CALCULATING FABRIC

1 Estimate the amount of fabric you will need by measuring the longest and widest point of the pad. Add 4 cm (1½ in) seam allowance in each direction.

2 Measure for the gusset approximately 10 cm (4 in) from the back of the pad along one side, across the front and along the other side to 10 cm (4 in) from the back. Add 2 cm (¾ in) either side of the width for seam allowance, and 4 cm (1½ in) to the length.

3 The rest of the gusset will need to be cut in two pieces so that the zip can be inserted along the centre. Cut two strips the length of the remaining gusset plus 4 cm (1½ in) seam allowance and two strips the width of the gusset plus 4 cm allowance for the zip and seam on each piece. Plan these pieces (top, bottom, gusset, and piping) on the work table to see how they fit into the fabric width, to prevent wastage.

4 If the fabric has a dominant pattern cut so that the pattern reads from front to back, following through the gusset.

1 Cut out pieces as planned, and make up the piping. Lay the front and back pieces onto the work table, right sides together. Cut balance marks on all four sides of the fabric, using single, double and triple cuts.

2 Starting on the back edge, pin piping (cord) to the right side of the fabric, all around the front and back pieces. Pin so that the stitching line on the piping casing is on the seam allowance. At the corners, snip right up to the stitching line on the piping, and open out the cut to a right angle so that the piping forms a tight corner. Pin securely from both sides and join (see Methods).

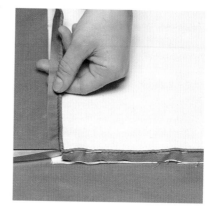

3 Stitch on piping. Make up the zip. Fold the two long sides of the gusset under 2 cm (¾ in) – if patterned make sure you fold the matching sides. Stitch one side of the zip onto one side of the gusset. The zip should be placed so that the slider is 2 cm (¾ in) in from one end and the zip end extends further than the gusset at the other end.

4 Pin the other side of the gusset along the zip, covering the teeth evenly. Stitch in place.

5 Stitch one end of the gusset to the slider end of the zip, with the zip closed. Open the zip slightly.

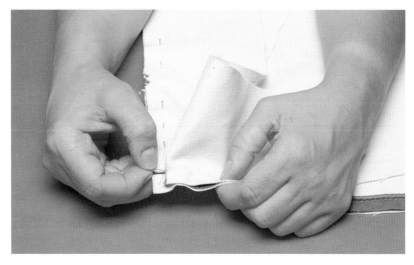

6 Starting with the free end of the gusset 10 cm (4 in) from the back, pin one side of the gusset to either the front or back of the cover. Match the seam allowance and pin onto the piping line. Cut into the corners, right up to the seam allowance to give a good square corner. Keep the cover flat on the work table and make sure that the two layers are equally pinned. Where the zip gusset and the main gusset meet, pin together and stitch the short seam before finishing the pinning. Cut away any excess fabric.

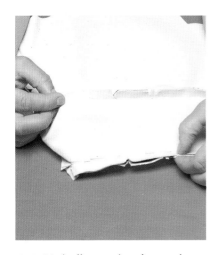

7 Stitch all around as close to the piping as possible. Pin the other side of the cover to the other side of the gusset. Starting at the back and matching the seam allowances, pin along the piping line. Match up the balance marks by scoring a pin line from a notch on the stitched side, across the gusset following the fabric grain. This should match the corresponding notch on the other piece of the cover. At each corner, score a pin line from the stitched corner to the opposite side of the gusset. Snip into the seam allowance, to form the corner. Stitch all around.

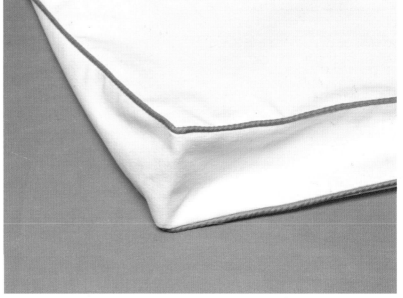

8 Trim the seam allowance to 1.5 cm (⅝ in). Cut across the corners to within 0.5 cm (¼ in) of the stitching. Neaten the seam and open up the zip. Turn the cover to the right side. Push into each corner with the end of your scissors to neaten. Press all over, lightly pressing the seam allowances away from the gusset. Fit pad into the cover, checking that each corner is well filled.

SQUAB CUSHION

Squabs fit onto wooden chair seats to make them more comfortable. They are made to fit the chair seat exactly. Instructions are given for a simple cover over a thin filling. A more substantial box cover, as illustrated below, can be made by combining the instructions here with those for box cushions (pp 66–67). Suitable fillings are horsehair pads, dacron-wrapped foam, or cotton wadding stitched into a pad. Pads are normally about 2.5 cm (1 in) deep but can be as much as 5 cm (2 in) deep if the chair seat needs lifting.

MATERIALS

newspaper or wallpaper
tape
pencil
foam cut to seat size (max depth 3 cm/ 1¼ in)
dacron to wrap around pad
curtain lining to cover both sides of pad
main fabric
fabric for ties and piping cord – contrasting if desired
zip
buttons (10–12 for each seat)

1 To make the template, cut a piece of newspaper or wallpaper larger than the seat. Secure on each side with tape. Fold the paper back onto itself around the back and legs, following the seat line, and tape in place. Cut around the leg, to the side of the seat. Mark the other sides with a pencil. Remove paper and cut to shape.

2 Cut out one piece of dacron to fit the seat pad exactly and place on top of the pad. Place the pad onto the remaining piece of the dacron, and fold up over the sides to meet the top piece. Feather out the dacron so that it clings to itself.

3 Cut out two pieces of lining using the template and adding half the side depth plus 1.5 cm (⅝ in) seam allowance all around. Make up four ties, and enough piping to go around the seat.
   With right sides together stitch around the leg cut-outs and three sides allowing 1.5 cm (⅝ in) for the seam. Turn right side out. Slip over the pad and slip stitch along the back.

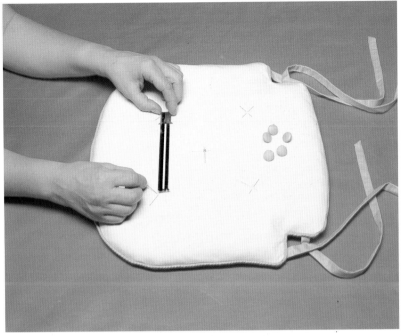

4 Use the template to cut out two pieces of fabric for the top and bottom of the squab, allowing 2.5 cm (1 in) for the seam. Pin the piping all around the top piece, snipping into curves and into the leg cut-outs, so piping lies flat.

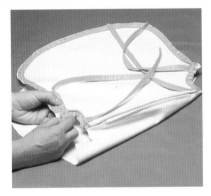

7 Stitch together and press. Slip the cover over the pad, making sure that the corners are well defined.

Mark button positions on both sides of the cushion.

5 Stitch the top piece to the bottom piece for 3 cm (1¼ in) along the back at each side. Sew in the zip by hand or machine. Position the ties to fit either side of the chair leg and stitch to secure.

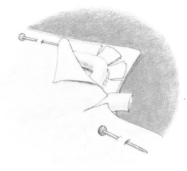

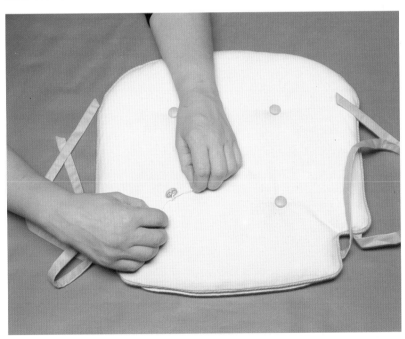

6 Undo the zip slightly. Pin the top piece to the bottom piece all around, along the seam allowance, pinning to the piping stitching line.

8 Use a heavy-duty needle and buttonhole or upholstery cotton and push through the pad from the bottom to the top. Thread through one button and back through the pad to within 3 mm (⅛ in) of the first hole. Tie together and pull the threads tightly. Knot two to three times to secure.

LOOSE COVERS

Loose covers, despite their name, are carefully fitted, and although the procedure may look complicated, with a little patience, attractive covers can be made as an alternative to upholstery.

Look at the chair or sofa you wish to cover. Take into account its function – is it a well-loved family sofa, or a decorative side chair? Consider the fabric – should it be plain or patterned? If you are attempting loose covers for the first time, make up a preliminary cover in calico, following the steps illustrated, and use as a pattern for cutting the main fabric.

Below A fresh and casual-looking cover is made up in cotton ticking, accented with green piping (cord). The green ties complete the relaxed, informal effect.

ARMCHAIR

The steps below illustrate how to cover a chair, but the procedure is identical for sofas.

CALCULATING FABRIC

1 View the chair as a series of rectangles: ie inside back; outside back; inside arm; outside arm; seat; front gusset; valance (dust ruffle); cushion pieces; arm cover.

2 Measure the chair for each of these pieces, allowing 3–4 cm (1¼–1½ in) seam allowance in each direction, plus 10–20 cm (4–8 in) for the 'tuck-in'. (Push your hand down into the chair around the seat, the inside arm and inside the wing to check the depth available for the tuck-in.)

3 Seams should never be in the centre of a cover. Always use a full width of fabric at the centre with panels joined to it at either side. Seams should always follow through from the front, across the seat and up through the back.

4 The pattern should be placed so that it is always the right way up. For this reason, the outside arm and the inside arm should never be cut as one piece. The pattern should match at each piping seam, and follow up through from the floor, across the seat and up the back. Cushions should always be made to match the position of the pattern on the main body of the chair or sofa cover.

5 Plan these pieces onto graph paper to make best use of the fabric width when estimating the amount needed. If you are using a patterned fabric, mark the graph paper into sections to show the repeat and the size of pattern. Cushions should be planned so that the backs and fronts are identical. For finishing ideas see p 75.

1 Cut out the pieces of fabric as planned. Make up the piping (cord) required for the whole job.

Using the tape measure, carefully position a vertical row of pins to mark the centre line of the inside back, outside back, front and seat of the chair.

Note: Loose covers are always cut for each chair individually – although two chairs might look the same, they very rarely are. The fabric must always be cut so that it is pinned in place with the right side out, as it will look when finished. Just as two chairs are never the same, neither are the left and right sides of any one chair identical.

2 Fold the inside back piece in half lengthwise, with the right sides of the fabric together. Finger press lightly. Line the fold line against the pinned centre line and pin at top and bottom. Open out the piece and pin at 10–20 cm (4–8 in) intervals to anchor to the side and top of the chair. Pins should be at right angles to the chair with the points inwards. Repeat with the outside back, anchoring the fabric to the sides and bottom of the frame as well.

Holding the fabric firmly between finger and thumb, pin the pieces together along the back edge of the chair. Remember that the pin line will be the seam/piping line so the pins must be positioned accurately. The pins should be positioned nose to tail, lying against the furniture to give an accurate line for stitching later. Start and finish 4–6 cm (1½–2½ in) above the arm on both sides, pinning from the back of the chair, and easing the front piece around any curves.

3 Fold over the top corner and pin. Cut away the excess fabric, leaving a 2 cm (¾ in) seam allowance. Cut single, double and triple V-shaped balance marks so that the pieces can be matched easily for stitching.

Unfold the top corner and pleat inwards. Using a small needle and double thread, ladder stitch along the fold line with tiny stitches. Fasten off securely at the corner of the chair back. Snip into this point from the side.

4 Position the inside and outside arm pieces of one arm onto the chair, checking the pattern is in the right place, and that the grain is straight vertically and horizontally. The pattern and grain of the outside arm should be level with the floor and not the top of the arm.

Pin these pieces together along the arm, making allowances for any curves. The seam may be at the top of the arm, on the outside of the arm or under the scroll, depending on the style of the chair. Repeat with the other arm.

7 Pin the outside arm pieces to the chair back piece from just below the arm to the bottom of the chair. At the top of one arm, fold the inside back piece up so that the fold line marks the eventual stitching line along the top of the arm, which will start at the seat and continue up around the arm to the back. Pin firmly to the back piece. Check that there are no wrinkles underneath the folded back fabric. Fold the inside arm piece back on itself in the same way, so that these two pieces meet at the back.

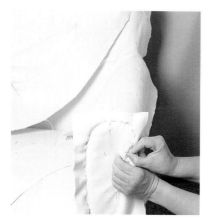

5 Pin the arm front to the chair, checking that the grain is straight. Fix the position with two crossed pins, and anchor all around, with pins at right angles to the chair, points inwards.

Pin the inside and outside arm pieces to the arm front piece, easing curves and fullness. Some arms will have no fullness to disperse, other arms will need one or two darts at this point, but usually the excess fabric will be eased in with small gathers or pleats, spread evenly around the curved section.

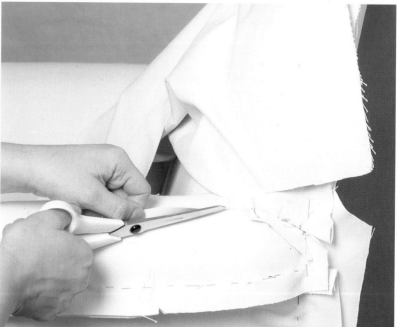

6 Trim away the excess fabric leaving a 2 cm (¾ in) seam allowance. Cut balance marks all around. Tack (baste) in contrasting thread to each piece at the actual meeting point of the arm seam and the arm front, and at any other area where they might be useful for matching the pieces before stitching. Repeat with other arm.

8 Pin the inside arm piece to the back piece.

Cut away the excess fabric to 3–4 cm (1¼–1½ in) seam allowance as far as the start of the curve of the arm and the seat back. Do not cut this too tightly in case some adjustment is needed later. Tack (baste) these two pieces three to four times along the folds at points exactly opposite each other so that the pieces can be matched accurately for seaming. Use contrasting thread and secure stitches – you do not want to risk these marks falling out.

Snip right into the seam allowance to allow the fabric to curve around the arm. Gradually cut the seam allowance back to 2 cm (¾ in). Take your time

over this stage, working with 2–3 cm (1½ in) of fabric around the curve at a time. Cut to the top of the inside of the arm and leave the fabric pinned back until the seat piece has been put in. Repeat with the other arm.

At the top of the arm, from the previous cut line, carefully fold back the inside arm piece and the inside back piece along the curve of the inside arm. Cut away the excess fabric, marking the opposite points with tacks as before.

Note: You might prefer to make a light pencil line along the folds if the chair has a difficult join, just to check that there aren't any unforeseen errors before cutting.

9 Place the seat piece onto the chair seat, matching the centre fold to the pinned line, as for the two back pieces. Anchor all around with pins, pointing into the seat. Fold the two sides over, along the length of the arms, so that the fold lines join the arm fronts at the edge of the front of the chair. Pin the front gusset to the front of the chair, checking that it is centred and level with the floor. Pin the top of this piece to the seat piece along the front edge.

Where these two pieces meet the arm front, push a pin through all three pieces so that there is a definite point at which they will meet when stitched. Mark each piece individually with a secure tack (basting stitch) in a contrasting colour at this point.

10 Pin the front gusset to both arm fronts, from the marked join to the bottom of both pieces. Measure and mark the folded-back sides of the seat piece so that the tuck-in is equal from front to back along the length of the arm. Cut along this line.

Pin the inside arm pieces to the seat piece for approximately 20 cm (8 in) from the front towards the back, cutting back and shaping the join to correspond with the available tuck-in allowance. (Push your hand into the side of the seat to check where the tuck-in will start and how deep it is at each point.)

11 Measure the tuck-in allowance and mark with pins onto the inside arm piece. Hold the inside arm piece and the inside back pieces together and cut the tuck-in allowance so that both sides are equal and the tuck-in at the bottom matches the tuck-in allowed on the seat. (To start with you might find this difficult. Because this area is out of sight, you can add in an extra section or make a gusset if you find this easier. Some arms are very hard to get absolutely perfect, and if all else fails a strategically placed cushion can cover an error.) Repeat with the other arm.

12 Using a 30 cm (12 in) ruler, measure up from the floor all around to the skirt position and mark with pins. Cut the excess fabric away leaving the seam allowance of 2 cm (¾ in). At this point, if the chair needs to have a back opening, fold back the outside arm piece and the back piece for the necessary fabric allowance. Pin the fabric back on itself to keep the fold. Mark the top of the opening with a tack (basting stitch) on each piece.

13 Tidy up and cut all seam allowances so that they are equal. Make sure that you have snipped enough balance marks. Use single, double and triple cuts to make matching easier.

Remove the anchor pins and lift the cover off. (See p 74 for instructions on making up loose covers.)

MAKING UP LOOSE COVERS

The following instructions will give a fairly tight cover, with the stitching line of the piping (cord) pinned along the seam allowance. If you want a looser cover, stitch with a smaller seam allowance than originally calculated. Make your own adjustments as preferred, as long as you are consistent throughout.

Do not unpin the whole cover at once. Work with small areas so there is a limited amount of fabric unpinned at any one time.

1 Take the pins from one of the seams joining the inside arm to the back, and turn the fabric inside out. Starting at the back, carefully match the tacks (basting stitches), and the ends of the easement cuts. Pin the seam down to the seat. Stitch, re-inforcing the curve line by stitching two rows very close together. Do not be afraid to stitch right next to the cuts – if you leave too much seam allowance the cover will not fit as well when replaced. Neaten the seam and repeat with the other side.

2 Next unpin one of the arm seams. If piping (cord) is to be used on the seam, pin the piping to the right side of the outside arm piece and stitch in place. Pin the inside arm to the piping line, right sides together, so that the seam allowances and notches match, and stitch. Position pins along the piping line and at right angles to it. The pins on this line will be removed as the machine approaches. Stitch as close to the piping as possible.

Pull the piping cord from inside the case at each end for 2 cm (¾ in). Cut the cord away so that the casing lies flat beyond the point at which the back and arm front seam meet. Repeat with the other arm.

3 Unpin the front gusset from the seat front. Turn inside out, pin the piping along the gusset piece and stitch. At the join with the arm front, pull and cut the cord as for step 2, so that the case is flat beyond the tack (baste) mark. Pin the right side of the seat piece to the piping line, matching seam allowance and notches. Stitch the length of the piping between the tack marks. Secure stitches firmly at each end. Neaten this seam.

4 One side at a time, unpin both sides of the seat from front to back. Turn inside out and pin together again, matching notches and seam allowance. Stitch from the front tack mark to the seam at the back. Neaten seams.

5 Unpin one of the front arms and turn inside out. Pin piping all around the arm, to the right side of the fabric, snipping piping at 1 cm (½ in) intervals to ease around the curve.

Stitch the piping in place. Pin the inside arm, outside arm and the front gusset to the arm front, matching seam allowances and balance marks. Stitch from the bottom of the front gusset up to the join with the seat, finishing with the needle in the tack mark. Secure with backwards and forward stitches to this point. Lift the cover away from the machine, fold over the seam, and start again, with the needle in the tack mark from the other side of the seam.

Stitch all around the cover, working on a small section at a time. Repeat with other arm.

6 Unpin the back piece. Pin piping to the right side of the fabric, along both sides and across the top. At the top corners, snip into the piping to allow it to lie flat, and stitch in place.

Pin the front to the back piece along the piping line. Use plenty of pins, pinned at right angles to the piping to ease any fullness. At the top corners make sure that the hand-stitched corners lie flat and that the finishing off stitches are inside the seam allowance. Stitch in place, as close to the piping as possible,

covering the previous stitching line. Stop the stitching at the top of the opening. Neaten the seam.

7 Slide the cover back onto the chair, and restitch any problem areas.

8 If the cover needs a back opening, cut a piece of the main fabric 16 cm (6½ in) wide and twice the length of the opening to make a placket. Stitch this piece to the right side of the cover on the back. Turn the cover and stitch down the other side. Press this piece into three and fold towards the inside, so that the fold line encloses the seam. Hand stitch to the stitching line. At the top of the opening, fold the placket in half and stitch across the width.

9 Pin piping on the seam allowance around the lower edge of the cover and stitch in place. At the back opening, pull and cut the cord as for step 2.

Pin valance (dust ruffle) onto the piping line all around the chair cover, stitch in place and neaten the seam. Fold the placket at the back over the seam and hand stitch in place.

10 Lie the back opening on a flat surface, and mark positions at approximately 10 cm (4 in) intervals to stitch hooks and thread bars. Stitch one hook just inside the piping on the back and make a thread bar on the valance (dust ruffle) at the other side to hold in place.

11 Press all seams, right side out, over a damp cloth. Press out cover and ease back onto the chair. Make sure that the seams all lie in the same direction. Ease the cover around curves and corners, finger pressing piping lines to straighten. You will need to spend time easing and fitting the cover into place on the chair, to obtain the best fit.

LOOSE COVER FINISHES

The following instructions are for variations on valances (dust ruffles) suitable for chairs or sofas.

> ### CALCULATING FABRIC
>
> 1 Measure the sides, front and back of the chair or sofa separately. Multiply these measurements by 2 to 2½ depending on the fullness required.
> 2 When you have decided on the depth, add seam allowances of 2 cm (¾ in) for the top, and 3 cm (1¼ in) for the hem.

FLAT, SHAPED VALANCE (DUST RUFFLE)

1 Measure the four sides of the chair. Cut a template of any shape – scallop, triangle, shells – in dimensions which fit easily into each of the four measurements. Cut out the main fabric following the template. Cut out a piece of lining the length of the main fabric and the depth of the widest point of the template. Pin together lining and main fabric, right sides facing, and stitch.

2 Cut the seam allowance down to 6mm (¼ in). Snip into any corners and curves. Turn right side out and press each seam as flat as possible and trim lining where necessary.

3 Pin onto the piping (cord) line on the cover. Stitch as close to the piping as possible, covering the previous stitching. Neaten the seam and press.

SIMPLE FRILL

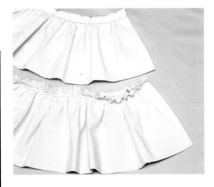

1 Calculate the fabric as described, and add 5 cm (2 in) for the overlap at the opening. Divide this figure by the width of the fabric, and cut the number of widths required. Cut the lining to the same dimensions.

Join seams and press flat. Pin main fabric and lining together along one long side. Stitch 1.5 cm (⅝ in) from the edge. Press seam towards the lining on the seam side.

2 Turn over and press along the seam from the right side. Fold so that 1 cm (½ in) main fabric is turned to the inside, and press. Pin top edge together at 20 cm (8 in) intervals and trim away any excess lining. Stitch a gathering thread 2 cm (¾ in) from the top edge.

3 Divide the length of the valance (dust ruffle) by ten and mark into ten sections with pins. Divide the total measurement of the chair sides by ten. Using this figure measure around and mark the piping (cord) line into ten sections.

4 Pin the valance sections to the chair cover sections. Pull up gathering threads and distribute fullness evenly within each section. Pin the valance to the piping line at right angles so that the pins can remain in place while machine stitching. Stitch all around as close to the piping as possible and neaten the seam.

BUTTERFLY FRILL

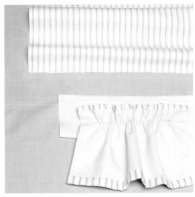

1 Decide the total depth of the frill to suit the chair and work out the fullness and widths of fabric needed as for a simple frill. Cut the main fabric to exactly the depth of the finished frill. Cut the backing fabric to this depth plus 7 cm (2¾ in).

2 Stitch the two pieces together, right sides facing along the length of the fabrics. Stitch the top line 1.25 cm (½ in) in from the edge and the bottom line 1.5 cm (⅝ in) in from the edge. Turn inside out.

3 Press seams towards the backing fabric. Neaten the short sides. Stitch a gathering thread along the top edge approximately 3.5 cm (1½ in) down. Divide the length by ten and mark into sections with pins. Divide the chair cover into ten equal sections. Pin the sections together so that the gathering thread is on the seam allowance. Pull up so that the fullness is distributed evenly. Stitch frill to the cover with a small zig-zag stitch to hold in place.

HIGH-BACKED CHAIR

This method can be used to cover dining chairs, or perhaps a chair in a study or at a dressing table in a bedroom. Choose appropriate fabrics and finishings. A tartan or check might be suitable for a masculine room treatment, while a floor length valance (dust ruffle) would look pretty in a bedroom (see p 75 for finishing ideas).

MATERIALS

main fabric

1.25 cm (½ in) tape for ties (approximately 6 metres/yards)

piping (cord)

2 cm (¾ in) tape to bind (approximately 2 metres/yards)

CALCULATING FABRIC

1 Measure the chair at the widest and highest points. Add 6 cm (2½ in) all around for seam allowances; 15 cm (6 in) for the tuck-in at the back of the seat, and 20 cm (8 in) for the flap under the chair seat.

2 Plan these pieces onto graph paper to calculate the fabric needed, allowing for the front, back, seat, valance (dust ruffle) and piping (cord), and taking into account any pattern repeat.

1 Cut pieces of fabric as planned and make up enough piping (cord) to go around the chair. Measure across the back and front of the chair and mark the centre lines with vertical rows of pins. Fold the front and back pieces of fabric in half lengthwise and finger press the centre line. (If the fabric is such that the press line will mark, measure and pin the centre line.) Position these pieces, one at a time, with the right side of the fabric facing out onto the chair, pinning the fabric pieces to the centre lines and

anchoring in place at approximately 12 cm (5 in) intervals all around.

Pin from the back of the chair. Holding the back and front pieces firmly between finger and thumb, pin together along the back edge. Start at the centre top and pin at approximately 12 cm (5 in) intervals. Pin back into these gaps, with the pins against the back edge to give a good stitching line. Pins should be nose to tail, giving a smooth line to follow.

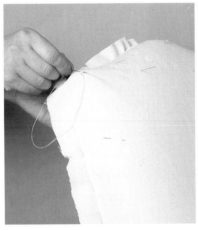

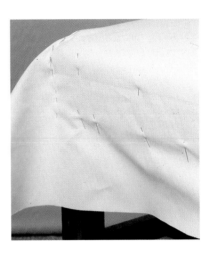

2 Pin the top corners into a dart. Cut away excess fabric to leave a 2 cm (¾ in) seam allowance. Snip balance marks at irregular intervals, making single, double and triple cuts so they can be easily identified. These marks will be used to match the back to the front once the pins have been removed, so are vital for the cover to fit well.

3 Unpin the top corners and fold fabric inside towards the top of the chair. Snip right into the seam allowance from the side, so that the fabric tuck will lie flat. Using double thread, ladder stitch the fold line, finishing off with a triple stitch at the corner, on the seam allowance.

4 Place the seat piece onto the chair seat, marking the centre line and anchoring all around as before. Pin the fabric into a dart at the front seat corners.

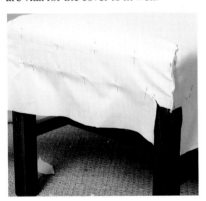

5 Trim away the seam allowance for the dart. Pin fabric to the lower edge of the chair seat all around. Use contrasting cotton to tack (baste) at the junction of the leg with the seat, and at the front and back corners.

Cut away the fabric to leave a 2 cm (¾ in) seam allowance around the leg. Snip at an angle into the tack point. Repeat with the other front leg.

6 At the back of the seat, fold the front piece back on itself so that the fold line forms the eventual stitching line which will join the seat to this piece. Make tack (baste) marks at 2 cm (¾ in) spaces along this line.

7 Push your hand into the back of the chair to find the depth available for the tuck-in allowance. Cut away fabric, leaving the 2 cm (¾ in) seam allowance from the chair back at the point where the tuck-in will start. Snip to the seam allowance at the innermost tack to allow the fabric for the tuck-in to lie flat on the chair seat with the side seam allowance still folded up.

Fold the back of the seat onto itself so that the fold matches the fold of the front piece and joins the innermost tack. Snip across the folded seat piece towards the tack on the front piece, so that both cuts meet at the seam allowance at the start of the tuck-in.

8 Pin the seat front to the chair back at each side. Fold the seat fabric down, from the cut to the chair back, so that the fold meets the folded seam allowance of the chair front. Tack (baste) exactly opposite the other tacking stitches, so that they will match up accurately for stitching. Trim away excess fabric leaving the 2 cm (¾ in) seam allowance. Pin the chair front and seat pieces together to make the tuck-in, and cut from the front of the tuck-in piece to the back at an angle, to allow the tuck-in to fit more easily.

9 Mark the back leg/seat join and cut away the back leg piece as for step 5. Measure down from the bottom of the seat, 13–15 cm (5–6 in). Cut away excess fabric, so that the flap is exactly the same depth all around.

10 Check that all seam allowances have been cut accurately and balance marks made. Remove all anchor pins and carefully take the cover off the chair.

MAKING UP

1 Work on one section at a time.

Unpin the seam between the seat and chair front on one side and enough of the back and tuck-in to allow you to work on this seam easily. Turn inside out. Match the tacked (basted) stitches together. Pin along the seam allowance. Stitch two lines closely together to reinforce. Stitch close to the end of the easement cuts so the join will not pull when the cover is on the chair. Repeat with the other seam. Undo the rest of the tuck-in and stitch.

Tack the darts on the front of the seat, and unpin. Turn inside out and pin back together along the tack line. Stitch carefully, tapering the dart away gently. Press on the right side, using a damp cloth to give a good finish.

Unpin the back and front pieces. Pin the piping all around the back piece, on the seam allowance, cutting right into the piping stitching line at the corner, and bending it around the corner to produce a sharp edge. Snip and ease where necessary. Stitch in place.

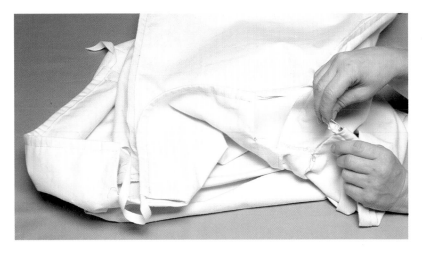

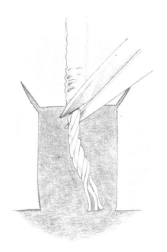

2 Pin the front to the back, matching the balance marks and the seam allowance. Pin into the corner so that the corner cut opens out and the dart lies flat. Pin the triple stitching right on the seam allowance at the corner of the piping. Pin at right angles across the piping to ease any fullness around the top curve. Stitch together.

At the back leg position, trim the piping level with the bottom of the fabric. Pull the cord from the piping case for 2 cm (¾ in). Cut away and pull back so that the piping case lies flat from the seam allowance to the bottom.

4 Make a 2 cm (¾ in) double hem on all four flaps, leaving the ends open. Using a large blunted needle or a safety pin, thread the 1.25 cm (½ in) tape through each of the pockets. To save pulling the tape out by mistake when you are working, attach a large safety

pin to the other end, and thread through a continuous loop. Pull approximately 1 metre (1 yard) of excess tape out at each corner, and cut off so that each corner has two 50 cm (18 in) tapes to tie around the legs.

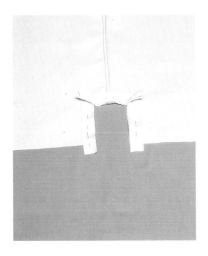

3 Stitch three pieces of tape over the raw edges, with the outside of the corners just on the edge of the cuts. Stitch around the outside edge. Press and fold under to the back, mitring the corners. Slip stitch the corners and the tapes to the chair cover.

5 Press the cover thoroughly. Ease onto the chair, finger pressing seams towards the back of the chair, and easing corners into position. Tie bows

under the seat at each leg and tuck the tapes inside the flaps. If necessary, press the cover again, when in position on the chair.

BEDROOM FURNISHINGS

All of the techniques explained in the previous chapters come together in the bedroom — unlined curtains will make gauzy bed drapes, pelmets (valances) can be made to go over a bedhead, and loose cover techniques can be used on headboards. Complete the look of luxury with a bed valance (dust ruffle).

Below A fresh and pretty bedroom treatment is achieved by combining the simplicity of white bedlinen with a valance (dust ruffle) and matching curtains.

BED VALANCE (DUST RUFFLE)

The primary function of a bed valance is to cover the part of the bed underneath the mattress. Traditionally, beds were made with a metal or wooden framework and were works of art in their own right – the same cannot be said of most modern divan beds. Bed valances can incorporate quite elaborate creations of fabrics, and may be gathered, box pleated, knife pleated, bound at the bottom, double frilled, gussetted and frilled – the possibilities are endless.

However the valance is designed, bear in mind that it should be lined, and full enough to give body. The skirt is attached to a main panel of fabric which holds it in place between the bed base and mattress.

MATERIALS

main fabric
lining for main fabric, plus enough to cover the bed base
fabric for binding or edging strips
piping (cord) to go around the top of the bed base
8 × 1.25 cm (½ in) ties, 50 cm (20 in) long to secure to the corners

CALCULATING FABRIC

1 Measure the bed base from the top to the floor. Note any unusual projections, bedposts, etc. which might prevent the valance (dust ruffle) fitting easily. Measure the length and width of the bed base for the main panel.
2 Measure the position of any bedhead fixings. Make a template of the corners at both the top and bottom ends of the bed base.
3 Decide on the length and fullness required. Allow enough to give a skirt of 2 to 2½ times fullness. Allow at least 1 cm (½ in) for the frilled skirt to drape to the floor.
4 Plan the widths of fabric needed. Allow 2 cm (¾ in) seam allowance all around the main panel and 6 cm (2½ in) for the skirt.

1 Cut the skirt widths of main fabric, join, and press seams flat. Repeat with the lining widths. Cut strips of fabric 15 cm (6 in) wide; two the length of the bed and one the width of the bed. Cut and join lining to length and width of the bed plus 2 cm (¾ in) seam allowance all around for the main panel.

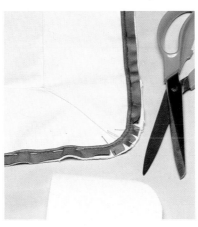

2 Press under 1.5 cm (⅝ in) all along one side of each of the strips for the bed base. Pin all three pieces on the main panel, with the outside raw edges level. Fold the side pieces back at the corners to mitre the joins. Stitch all around the inside of these strips.

3 Place the corner template onto the main panel and cut around, allowing for seam allowance. Following the template, shape corners and pin piping (cord) all around the pieces for the two sides and bottom of the bed, and for approximately 15 cm (6 in) around the top corners of the fabric for the head of the bed.

4 Stitch the skirt lining to the skirt fabric, right sides together, with a 1.5 cm (⅝ in) seam allowance. Press from the front, pressing the fabric towards the lining. Turn over and press.

5 Press the lining up so that the fabric is folded underneath by approximately 2.5 cm (1 in). Pin all along the top edge and trim lining to match the main fabric.

6 Press the short ends of fabric and lining in and slip stitch together. Stitch a double gathering thread all around, 1.5 cm (⅝ in) and 2 cm (¾ in) from the top edge. Measure all around the piping on the main panel and divide by ten, and mark the main panel into ten equal sections.

Measure the skirt accurately and also divide by ten, and pin the skirt to the main panel at the marked points. Pull the threads to gather each section and distribute the gathers evenly. Pin the gathering line to the piping line.

7 To finish, stitch the skirt to the main panel, and neaten the seam. Stitch two ties to each corner. Press thoroughly. Lift the mattress from the bed, place the valance on top of the bed base and fix the ties around the bed legs to keep the valance in place.

FITTED HEADBOARD

A fitted headboard is made on much the same lines as loose covers. The instructions are given for a fairly tight-fitting cover. Adjust the seam allowances for a looser fit.

MATERIALS

1 headboard covered in calico
main fabric
piping (cord)
6 to 12 × 1.25 cm (½ in) ties, 25 cm (10 in) long

CALCULATING FABRIC

Measure the widest and highest points of the headboard to estimate the fabric needed. If the headboard is wider than the width of your fabric, allow two widths of fabric times the height of the headboard. Allow seam allowances of 6 cm (2½ in) for the length and 8 cm (3 in) for the height of the headboard.

1 Measure carefully across the headboard and mark the centre with a vertical row of pins.

Make up enough piping (cord) to go around the headboard. Fold the front fabric in half and finger press the centre fold (this will not form a crease, but will show you the centre line).

Position front fabric onto the headboard, lining up the centre fold with the pinned line and transferring the pins from the headboard to hold the fabric. Anchor in place along the

centre line and at intervals of approximately 15 cm (6 in) around the headboard top and sides.

Pin pieces together from the back, as for loose covers (see pp 70–71) easing any fullness into tiny gathers so that the front fabric does not pull. Fold the top corner into a dart on the right side, or ease if curved, and pin down both sides. Trim away the excess fabric to leave a 2 cm (¾ in) seam allowance. Snip balance marks at intervals around the cover.

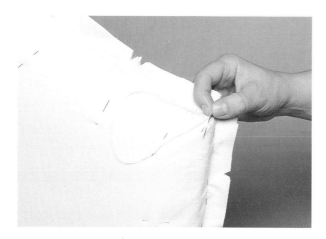

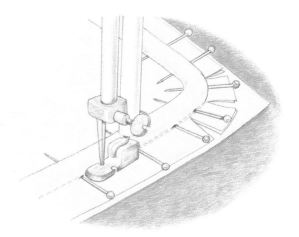

2 Unpin the dart at the top corner and fold under. Fold the fabric to the top of the headboard. Snip into the corner almost up to the seam allowance from the side of the front cover piece, so that the fabric tuck lies flat. Pin in place. With a small needle and double thread, hand stitch the corner 'dart' with tiny ladder stitches. Finish off with several stitches on the seam allowance at the corner point of the headboard.

3 Remove the cover and all pins. Pin piping all around the back piece, so that the front of the piping is on the seam allowance. This allows some slight easement when the cover is fitted.

Snip right into the stitching line on the piping at the top corner. Pin at each side of the corner to prevent the piping moving with pins at right angles to anchor it while stitching. Stitch in place.

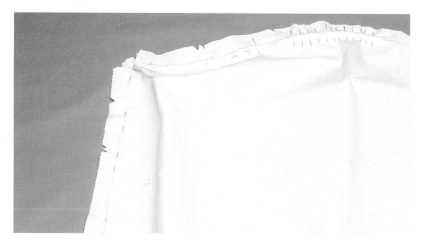

4 Pin the front piece to the back piece along the piping stitching line, matching balance marks and seam allowances. The finishing off stitches must fit right into the corner, with the corner cut opened out so the corner lies flat.

Use pins at right angles to the piping to ease gathers around shaped sections. These pins will remain in place while stitching to prevent fabric puckering.

Stitch around the headboard as close to the piping as possible. Stitch slowly over the holding pins to prevent the needle breaking, and remove the other pins as you approach them. Check from the right side that the previous stitching line is not visible. If it is, re-stitch (without the pins) from the same side, just inside the last stitching line.

5 At the bottom of both sides, pull the piping 4 cm (1½ in) from its casing. Cut away and pull back so that the casing lies flat from the seam allowance to the edge. Turn fabric over 2 cm (¾ in), twice, to form the hem. Pin ties in at intervals (avoiding leg positions) and stitch all around.

6 Press the cover and ease back onto the headboard. Finger press all seam allowances in the same direction and tie at lower edge.

PADDED HEADBOARD

A padded, buttoned headboard will add a touch of easy comfort in a bedroom, and is quite simple and inexpensive to make. It is filled with a duvet (continental quilt), and is easily removed for washing.

MATERIALS

main fabric
1 duvet (continental quilt)
lining fabric to cover the board
4 to 8 × 1.25 cm (½ in) tapes for bottom ties, 25 cm (10 in) long
8 × 2.5 cm (1 in) tapes for side ties, 40 cm (16 in) long
drill
1 piece of board the width of the bed, 40–65 cm (16–20 in) high
thin cord or buttonhole thread
2–4 toggles
2–4 large buttons

---

1 Make up a lining for the board. This may either be glued onto the board or made up as a slip cover. The last 20 cm (8 in) of each side should be covered in the main headboard fabric, but the centre panel can be lining fabric or any other white or self-coloured piece of fabric. This will be fitted to the board once the holes have been drilled.

2 Cut a fibre duvet (continental quilt) to size, adding 10 cm (4 in) to the length and width of the headboard. Stitch the cut ends closed.

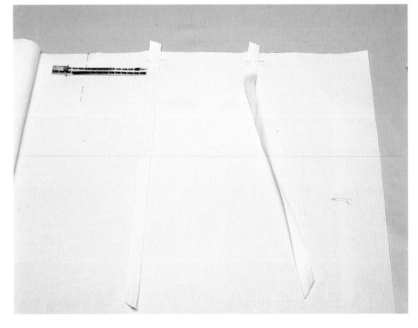

3 Cut two pieces of the main fabric to these measurements plus seam allowances of 4 cm (1½ in) lengthwise and 6 cm (2½ in) widthwise.

Place one piece onto the work table, right side up and mark the centre of each side. Pin four ties along the side, 10–20 cm (4–8 in) and 20–40 cm (8–16 in) either side of the centre mark.

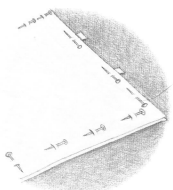

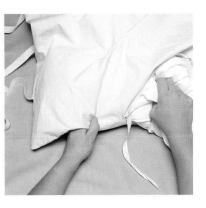

4 Place the other piece on top of the first, right sides together. Pin along the two sides, securing the ties, and along the seam allowance on the top, 2 cm (¾ in) in from the edge. Pin along the seam allowance on the bottom, 4 cm (1½ in) in from the edge, and 20–40 cm (8–16 in) in from each side, depending on the size of the cover.

5 Stitch and press. Cut away the four corners at right angles. Turn fabric under 2 cm (1 in) twice, along the bottom edge of each piece. Pin 1.25 cm (½ in) ties at 25–30 cm (10–12 in) intervals along both sides, exactly opposite each other. Tuck the raw edge into the fold, and turn the tape over so that it is pinned in place, falling towards the bottom of the headboard cover.

6 Stitch the turning and tapes in position. Press seams flat from the wrong side. Turn the cover right side out, and press seams so that they lie flat. Fill the cover with the duvet (continental quilt), making sure that it goes right into the corners.

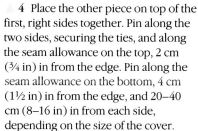

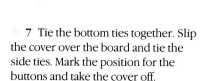

7 Tie the bottom ties together. Slip the cover over the board and tie the side ties. Mark the position for the buttons and take the cover off.

Drill one or two holes in the board to coincide with the button position. Fit the lining onto the board, cutting holes for button positions.

Thread a large needle with thin cord or buttonhole thread and stitch from the front to the back of the quilted cover. Tie the thread around a toggle at the back, bring the thread through to the front and through the button. Tie the two ends of the thread together without pulling it tight. The button and toggle should be tight enough to make a slight indentation in the duvet (continental quilt). Repeat this on the front and back of the cover at each button position.

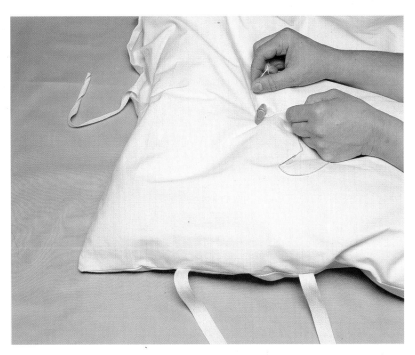

8 Slip the cover over the board again. Push the front toggle through the hole and leave at the back. Push the back toggle through the hole and leave at the front. Repeat with the other set of buttons and toggles. The toggles should now be pulling quite tightly. Tie the side ties into bows.

TABLECLOTHS

 Decorative tablecloths or table covers are quite simple to make and can transform an awkward corner, or liven up an uninteresting room in no time. For a study, or room with heavy furniture, use fabrics such as heavy wool, crushed velvet, brocade or damask with rope or fringed hems. Use pretty chintz fabrics with bound or frilled hems for a light room or bedroom. Inexpensive fabrics can be used as undercloths for antique shawls and calico may be embellished with a hand-painted stencil around the hemline to create an individual style.

Below The bright mix of Provençal-print tablecloths is perfectly suited to this appealing country kitchen and the cloths themselves are very simple to make.

SQUARE CLOTHS

Square or rectangular cloths are the easiest soft furnishings to make, but the effect of two or three layers of cloths in complementary fabrics, with napkins and colourful china, can turn any table into a visual feast. Kitchen cloths should be made just 15–20 cm (6–8 in) longer than the tabletop, so that the overhang is not fussy. Dining cloths should be more elegant – an overhang to the top of the seats or to the floor is more appropriate.

Make a simple rectangular undercloth to protect the dining table surface, and cover with chenille or old tapestry for everyday use. A rectangular cloth may be used as a permanent fixture, to cover an unattractive heat-resistant cover, with decorative dining cloths reserved for suppers and special occasions.

For pretty kitchen and outdoor cloths, choose four to five fabrics which work well together and make two undercloths which will cover the whole table and overhang. Make up three square cloths which can be set at angles over the undercloths, and easily removed for cleaning, and use the same fabrics to make up a mixture of colourful napkins. There will always be enough clean linen to lay an attractive table at very short notice – and even bread and cheese will taste wonderful on such a pretty table.

CALCULATING FABRIC

1 Measure the length and width of your table. Add 15–20 cm (6–8 in) for the overhang at each side and 3 cm (1¼ in) each side for the hems. Decide whether you will need to join your fabric or whether the cloth will fit into the width. If your measurements are only just over the fabric width you could consider reducing the overhang slightly to avoid wasting fabric.

2 If you do have to join widths, add equal panels either side of the centre width to avoid a centre seam.

3 Allow a minimum of 35 cm (14 in) for napkins. These will be on the small side, so only suitable for cakes or breakfast. Plan to cut three napkins across the width if your fabric is 135 cm (54 in) wide. With 1.5 cm (⅝ in) turnings all around you will end up with napkins approximately 42 cm (17 in) square. If you want larger napkins allow to cut two across the width of fabric.

1 Cut and join fabrics as planned. Make small French seams so that there are no raw edges.

2 Press each side 3 cm (1¼ in) to the wrong side. Cut away the corners at an angle to within 0.5 cm (¼ in) of the fold line. Press each side in 1.5 cm (⅝ in). Mitre the corners. Pin all around and stitch in place with matching or toning cotton.

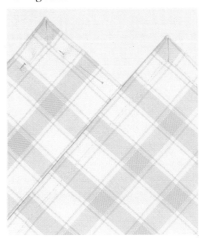

HEM FINISHES
a) Make turnings as below, but stitch all around in very close satin stitch in a contrasting colour.
b) Make turnings and satin stitch as above. Stitch another row of satin stitch in another contrasting colour approximately 0.5–1 cm (¼–½ in) inside the first row.
c) If the fabric is suitable to make a frayed edge, zig zag stitch all around the napkin approximately 2.5 cm (1 in) in from the edge. Working with one side at a time, pull the threads away until you meet the stitching and no more threads will pull away.

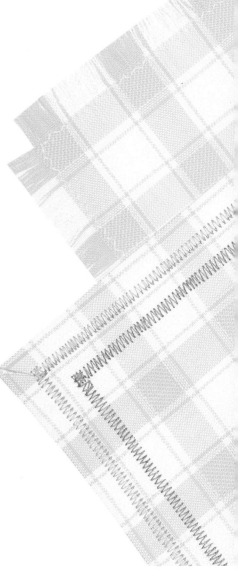

ROUND CLOTHS

Round cloths are particularly attractive when used on bedside tables, and can be as decorative or as plain as the bedroom design allows. Always allow enough fullness with frilled edgings to allow frills to drape onto the floor. If you happen to find an old bedside cupboard in a junk shop, a table top can be cut to size and fitted to the cupboard top. Use a coat of paint to freshen up, embellish with a pretty cloth, and make a sturdy, useful bedside table at very little expense.

CALCULATING FABRIC

1 To find the diameter of the cloth, measure the height and width of the table. Add the height × 2 to the width.
example
60 cm + 50 cm + 60 cm
(24 in + 20 in + 24 in)

2 Measure the drape required and add the difference to the above
example
2 cm + 60 cm + 50 cm + 60 cm + 2 cm = 174 cm
(1 in + 24 in + 20 in + 24 in + 1 in = 70 in)

3 Add turning allowance of 3 cm (1 in) all around

4 To calculate the number of lengths of fabric needed, divide this measurement by the width of the fabric.
example
180 cm ÷ 135 cm = 1.3
(72 in ÷ 54 in = 1.3)

Two widths of fabric will be needed.

5 If using a patterned fabric, calculate the cut lengths needed for an accurate match by dividing the length by the pattern repeat.
example
180 cm ÷ 50 cm = 3.6
(72 in ÷ 20 in = 3.6)

Allow to the next full pattern repeat and multiply by the length of the repeat.

6 Multiply this by the number of fabric widths required to obtain the amount of fabric needed.

1 Cut the fabric into the two lengths as estimated. Fold one in half lengthways and cut along the fold line. Join these half widths to the whole width, at either side, matching the pattern as necessary. Press seams flat and cut away the selvedge and selvedge writing.

2 Lightly fold this joined piece in half lengthwise and then widthwise, keeping the edges straight and the seams on top of each other. (If the fabric is glazed, be especially careful not to press the folds or it will cause the glaze to crack.)

3 Using a ruler and plenty of pins, measure from the corner out to half of the diameter and mark with a pin. Continue all around the quarter circle, pinning at no more than 5 cm (2 in) intervals.

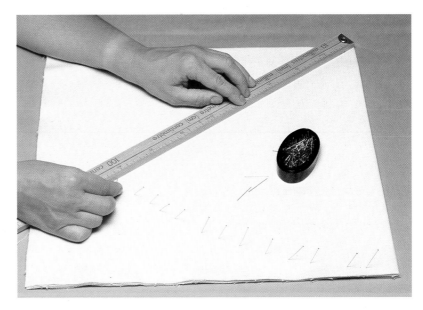

4 Cut along this pin line, through all thicknesses. Open out the circle of fabric and place face down onto the work table. Press the hem allowance up all around, pinning approximately every 2 cm (¾ in) with the pins at right angles to the hemline. These pins will ease the inevitable fullness and keep the hemline even. Herringbone all around to hold the hem in place, with no visible stitching on the front.

Note: If interlining is to be used, follow the instructions above, laying the interlining over the main fabric and locking in place at each seam and across each width three times. Fold over the hem allowance and press. Cut away the interlining along the fold line.

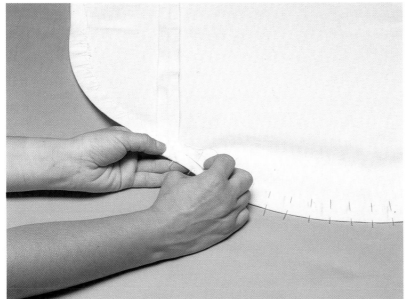

5 Make up the lining as main fabric. Place over the table cloth, wrong sides together. Lock the lining to the cloth along the seams.

6 Cut away the excess lining overhanging the circumference. Score along the hemline with the point of the closed scissors and follow this line. Press the lining under 1.5 cm (⅝ in). Pin in place and slip stitch all the way around leaving a neat 1.5 cm (⅝ in) of main fabric showing.

METHODS

To make up soft furnishings successfully, you need to know a few basic sewing techniques. The following pages explain the stitches, seams and tricks of the trade used in the projects throughout this book.

CUTTING FABRIC

1 Check for flaws. There will almost certainly be flaws in a large quantity of fabric so marking them now will enable you to plan around them. If you have flaws which are unacceptably noticeable, arrange to exchange the fabric. Manufacturers will not accept responsibility once the fabric has been cut.

2 Check that the pattern is not 'off grain'. The allowed tolerance is 3 cm (1¼ in) but if it is more than 1 cm (½ in) 'off grain' you may want to return the fabric.

3 If the right side of the fabric or direction of the pattern is not obvious, use tacks (basting stitches) or pins to mark each piece as it is cut.

4 Cut away selvedges and any writing on printed fabrics. Snip into selvedges to allow some seam easement if fabric reacts to atmospheric changes.

5 Cut carefully and evenly across the width, with fabric square to the selvedge. Leave pieces overnight to stabilise, with as few folds as possible.

STITCHES

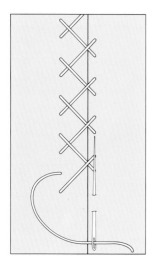

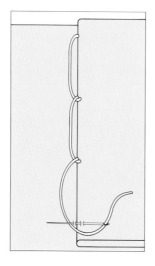

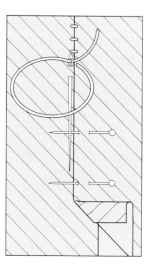

Invisible tacking

This stitch will enable you to join fabric from the right side, essential for matching patterns. Fold under seam allowance on one piece of fabric, and place over the other, matching patterns exactly. Pin in place. Starting under the folded edge, move the needle across into the flat piece of fabric. Make a 2 cm (¾ in) stitch under the seamline, and then move back across the join, taking a stitch into the two layers of fabric. Continue moving back and forth across the join, stitching down the seamline and back into the two layers of fabric. When completed, right sides may be folded together and machine stitched.

Herringbone stitch

This is a crossed stitch used to hold hems in place. Bring the thread up through the hem 3 mm (⅛ in) below the edge. Move the needle diagonally to the right, and take a stitch from right to left just above the hem edge. Bring the needle down again diagonally and repeat, to make crossed stitches along the edge of the hem.

Locking-in

This is a loose, looped stitch, used for interlined curtains to hold the interlining to the curtain fabric. Pin interlining to main fabric, wrong sides together. Fold the lining back against the pins. At right angles to the folded edge, stitch through the edge and main fabric, picking up one or two threads only with each stitch. Move the needle about 5 cm (2 in) to the right, over the thread to produce a loop. Do not pull tight.

Ladder stitch

This stitch is used to sew folded edges together. With folded edges flush, start at one edge, and cross horizontally over the opening into the opposite edge. Make a short stitch and move needle back across to the other edge. Make a short stitch in this edge. Repeat back and forth across the opening.

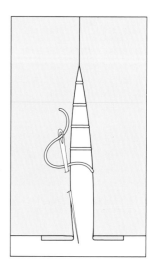

SEAMS

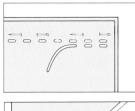

Flat seam

With right sides pinned together, machine stitch inside the raw edge (usually about 2 cm/¾ in). Remove pins and press seam allowance flat from the back. Turn over and press from the front, over a slightly damp cloth.

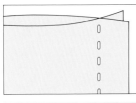

French seam

This seam encloses the raw edges of the fabric, and is often used on lightweight fabrics when an untidy edge might be visible. Pin wrong sides of fabric together, and stitch about 6 mm (¼ in) from the edges. Refold with right sides together, pin and stitch again just beyond the first stitching line to enclose the raw edges.

PINNING

Pins should be positioned to follow the seam allowance exactly, with the body straight and the heads pointing away from the direction that the machine will approach. The pins will be removed one at a time to allow the stitching line to take their place. Pins should also be pinned at right angles to the stitching line at 5–10 cm (2–4 in) intervals. These will remain in place while stitching to prevent the layers of fabric moving.

A neat line of pins will provide guidance for a straight stitching line and will result in a more professional finish. Take time over pinning to ensure the line is straight.

TIES

To make ties, cut pieces of fabric to the required length and four times the finished width. Fold in half lengthwise, right sides inside, enclosing a piece of cord which is longer than the strip of fabric. Stitch along the short side, securing the cord firmly, and along the length, just away from the centre towards the raw edges.

Cut across the corner. Pull the cord through and turn fabric right side out. Cut off the cord and the end. Press and turn the raw edges under at one end and handstitch together.

PUTTING IN A ZIP

1 Open up the zip fully. Press under 2 cm (¾ in) of the fabric, the length of the zip. Pin this to one side of the zip and stitch as close to the teeth as possible.

2 Close up the zip. Fold the seam allowance under on the opposite piece of fabric. Place over the zip so that the previous stitching line is not visible. Pin to the zip, close to the opposite teeth and stitch in place.

MAKING PIPING (CORD)

Piping does not always need to be cut on the cross. If the lines to be piped are straight then the piping may also be straight.

It is important that you have a piping or zipper foot which will allow you to stitch very close to the cord. If not, the casing will wrinkle, whether or not the piping is cut on the cross.

Cut the lengths as long as possible to prevent unnecessary joins. Always cut the ends across and join the lengths across the widths. Joining on the straight will cause a thicker join with four layers of fabric being stitched together into the seam.

JOINING PIPING (CORD)

1 Start to pin the piping to the main fabric at a point which will not be obvious when the article is made up.

2 Cut the other end of the piping approximately 3 cm (1¼ in) beyond the joining position.

3 Unpick the casing back to 2 cm (¾ in) beyond the joining position. Cut the inside cord away so that the two pieces butt up.

4 Fold the raw edge in 1 cm (½ in). Fold this piece over the first piece and pin to secure. Double stitch over the join.

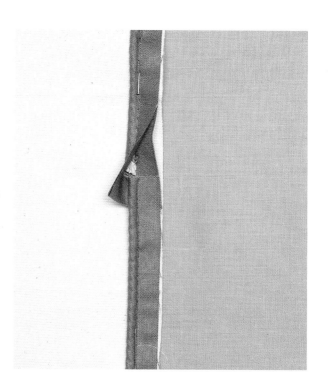

PINNING PIPING (CORD) ONTO THE FABRIC

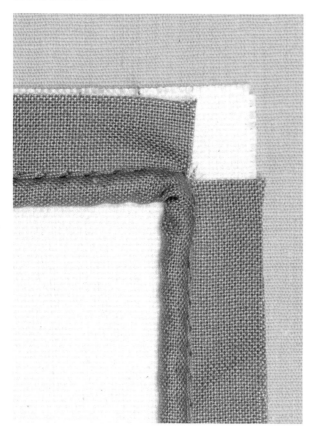

Corners

Stop pinning at the seam allowance before each corner. Snip right into the stitching line, and fold the piping sharply to make a 90° angle and pin around the corner.

Curves

Snip into the piping line around inward curves to allow the casing to overlap and the piping to lie flat. If the fabric is bulky cut out V shapes.

For outward curves, snipping into the casing will allow it to spread and accommodate the curve.

PATTERN MATCHING

1 Lie one of the cuts face up onto the work table, approximately 20 cm (8 in) in from the long side. Hold in place with curtain clamps.

2 Press the selvedge and a small amount of the pattern to the wrong side of the piece which is to be joined to the first length.

3 Lay this piece carefully onto the first, pinning the pattern so that it matches accurately.

4 Using single thread, weave in and out with 1 cm (½ in) stitches, tacking (basting) the two pieces together accurately.

5 Remove pins. Fold back the other side and pin at right angles to the selvedge to secure.

6 Stitch along the tacked and folded line, leaving the pins to prevent the fabric moving away from the match. Turn over to right side and press along the stitching line with an iron over a slightly damp cloth.

CARE AND CLEANING

Some soft furnishings are more easily cleaned than others, but all will benefit from regular care and upkeep. The following tips will ensure your fabrics look their best.

WASHING

Unlined curtains will usually require regular cleaning. These may be washed or dry cleaned in accordance with manufacturers' instructions. If frequent washing is essential, make up curtains in a strong hardwearing fabric like cotton, with enough substance to stand regular handling. To prevent a shrinkage problem, either wash the fabric *before* making up or over-cut the drops, and make up with the shrinkage allowance. This will be taken up at the first wash.

When washing by hand or machine, make sure that every trace of detergent is removed. Sunlight will react with the chemicals and cause the fabric to fade.

Always press while still damp. If you do have a shrinkage problem, pressing and steaming can sometimes pull the fabric back into shape. Never press over seams, but press up to them with the point of the iron. If you do need to press over a seam, slip a piece of cloth between the seam and the main fabric to prevent a ridge forming.

To clean loose covers, follow the manufacturers' instructions for washing the fabric, and half dry as recommended. Press into the seams from either side, taking care not to press over the seams which will leave a ridge in the main cover. Ease the cover back onto the chair or sofa while still damp and finger press all the seams in the same direction – usually to the back and downwards, although sometimes the shape of the chair demands otherwise. Pull the cover into shape over curves and corners.

AIRING

The best and most effective way to keep curtains clean and fresh is to choose a slightly breezy day, open the windows wide, close the curtains and allow them to blow in the wind for a few hours. This will remove the slightly musty lining smell. If you can do this every few weeks your curtains will stay 'fresh'. This may pose a problem in the city, but if you choose a quiet, breezy Sunday, you should be able to give your curtains more than just an occasional airing.

VACUUMING

Remove dust regularly to prevent it settling into the fabric grain. Once dirt has penetrated it is very difficult to remove. Vacuum your soft furnishings regularly with a soft brush attachment. Pay special attention to the inside of chair seats, pleats in headings and lampshades, swagged drapes, pelmets (valances), frills and edgings. Use the vacuum brush in line with the drape, and not across the grain. For delicate fabrics and pelmets, make a muslin or fine calico 'mob cap', elasticated to fit over the end of the brush. This will soften abrasion between the bristle and fabric.

SPECIAL CARE

Some fabrics and small furnishings such as silk cushions will need cleaning at some stage. Use a specialist furnishings dry cleaner and clean before dirt is ingrained.

Interlined curtains should never be cleaned unless a disaster makes cleaning absolutely necessary. Regular care and attention as suggested above will prevent curtains from becoming 'dirty'.

If curtains need to be altered for any reason (like moving house) have them cleaned by a specialist dry cleaner before alterations are carried out. Remove stitching from the sides and hems to allow any wrinkled fabric to be cleaned and to allow the fabrics to shrink at different rates.

TRACK (ROD) MAINTENANCE

Periodically spray the inside of curtain tracks and the top of poles with an anti-static household cleaner or silicon spray to prevent dust building up and to ease the running. Poles may be cleaned with a diluted household cleaner and a soft brush to remove dust from the crevices of decorative finials and the underside of curtain rings.

STOCKISTS

All fabrics used throughout this book are available from **Calluna Ltd**, The Coach House, Hill House, Creech St Michael, Taunton, Somerset TA3 5DP, United Kingdom (tel 0823 442711)

UNITED KINGDOM

Bennison Fabrics, 16 Holbein Place, London SW1, 071 730 8076
The Bradley Collection, The Granary, Flowton Brook, Flowton, Suffolk IP8 4LJ, 0473 87651 (curtain fittings)
Wendy Cushing, 253 Fulham Road, London SW3, 071 739 5909 (curtain fittings)
Colefax & Fowler, 118 Garratt Lane, London SW18, 081 874 6484
Designers Guild, 271 & 277 Kings Road, London SW3, 071 351 5775
DG Distribution, 26 Old Church St, London SW23, 071 352 3111
Fired Earth, Twyford Mill, Oxford Road, Adderbury, Oxfordshire, 0295 812088
George Spencer, 4 West Halkin Street, London SW1, 071 235 1501
Kirsch, Hallis Hudson, Bushell Street, Preston PR1 2SP, 0772 202202 (tracks and fittings)
Hill & Knowles, 13 Mount Road, Feltham, Middlesex, TW13 6AR, 081 893 2101

UNITED STATES

Curtains & Home, 1600 Old Country Road, Plainview, NY, (800) 643-2143
Home Depot, 2727 Paces Ferry Road, Atlanta, GA 30339, (404) 433-8211
R. H. Macy & Company, 151 West 34th Street, New York, NY 10001, (800) 222-6161
Maharam Vertical Surfaces, P.O. Box 6900 Hauppauge, NY 11788
Montgomery Ward, 1 N.W. Plaza, Chicago, Ill 60671
J. C. Penney, 1301 Avenue of the Americas, New York, NY 10019, (800) 222-6161
Pier One Imports, 301 Commerce Street, Fort Worth, TX 76102, (817) 878-8000
Sears Roebuck, Sears Tower, Chicago, Ill 60684, (800) 366-3000
Shears & Windows, 101 Henry Adams Street, San Francisco, CA 94901 (415) 621-0911

PICTURE CREDITS

The author and publishers would like to thank **Laura Ashley**, for permission to reproduce the images on pages 22 and 28; and **Today Interiors** for the images on pages 2, 42 and 60.

ACKNOWLEDGEMENTS

My thanks and gratitude to all those without whom this book would not have been written.

To Joanna and Lindsay at Anness Publishing who have worked so hard to produce this book; to John whose continual enthusiasm, patience and attention to detail have given such clear and inspiring photographs; to my assistant Charlotte; to Sarah, Julie, Jacky and Lisa for their expertise and help in making up the projects.

Special thanks to my husband, Don, and my teenagers Peter, Michael and Lisa for their support and understanding.

I am indebted to my friends, David and Elizabeth, David and Imogen, and Johnny and Jano for their generosity in allowing us to share their homes.

INDEX